Joel McKerrow's beautifully written n[...] *to my own as I have wrestled with reco[...]* *me. The language and perspective he b[...]* *....y of us as we* *find ourselves in either a measure of certainty, an unravelling, or a weaving* *back together. Joel's story reminds us that questioning, doubt and despair,* *as well as beauty, trust and joy, are necessary for a transformed life.*

Vickie Reddy
Executive Producer, The Justice Conference; Founder, SPARC

This book is not for the faint-hearted. But then nothing worth doing is *ever easy. You will be called, alongside Joel, to explore your own half-lies* *and restlessness. You will also be called to journey from the known to the* *unknown. You will not find in this a voyeuristic, self-indulgent narrative.* *Rather you, like Joel, may find yourself arriving at a destination that* *involves a tradition and a tribe.*

Justin Duckworth
Anglican Bishop of Wellington, NZ

Woven is about the deepest aches of the earth, and the grief of the human *soul ... This is a book for those who have grown up religious and who* *fear that they cannot hear the still small whisper any longer. It is also a* *book for people who dislike Christian hypocrites, and need to hear that* *the Christian God is a lion who roars for justice in the face of poverty and* *global turmoil ... If you've ever felt unravelled and needed to pull all the* *threads together or just asked 'where are you God?' (or known someone* *who has) then this is the right book.*

Tanya Riches
Senior Lecturer and Masters Program Coordinator, Hillsong College

Woven is a magnificent work-of-the-heart tapestry: its weave includes *profound reflection on the stages of faith, along with personal and social* *insights, stories of deep reverential humanity, a strong sense of place in the* *natural world and the still small irresistible voice of God. It is all there. It is* *gifted poetry in prose and prose in poetry. This is a book to savour. Indeed, it is a testament of mellowing into a contemplative faith and the influence of other Christian thinkers and mystics in carrying the torch to light the way. It is undoubtedly a fresh Christian classic from a voice much needed in our times.*

Tim Costello
Executive Director, Micah Australia

Over a hundred years ago, William James described what he termed the twice-born soul – the person who had found a richer, more sustaining faith by going through the painful loss of childhood belief. He said the faith of the twice-born is more robust, like a bone that breaks and heals stronger at the broken place. This beautifully written book is for those who have chafed at the loss of faith and hunger to be twice-born. Joel McKerrow leads us gently but insistently through the grief of losing our religion to the less cheerful, less confident, deeper, more realistic outlook of what he calls the woven self. This is a brave, honest, and heart-warming book.

Michael Frost
Morling College, Sydney

Through Woven, *master poet Joel McKerrow leads readers on pilgrimage through his own epic journey from encounter with soul-rattling truth, through consequent unravelling to confrontation with a depth of grace, love, beauty and kinship previously unimaginable to him. This is one man's story and simultaneously it is the story of the movement of the Spirit across the Western Church – a movement of reckoning, repentance and re-formation.*

Lisa Sharon Harper
Writer and Speaker; Founder and President, Freedom Road, LLC

Deep, true, painful, honest, hopeful, vulnerable, strong ... If you are wondering if there is more, if truth would lead you somewhere, if you'd do something wonderful when you aren't so afraid, then this book is an invitation to a deeper life and a journey guide to wholeness. Maybe you are undone by injustice, tired of the endless pursuit of freedom, overcome by the darkness, you'll find this book a balm for your wound and hope for your sails. Anywhere you are on life's journey, this book is a great place to stop and inhale the truth that will lead you home.

Danielle Strickland
Speaker, Author, Advocate

Amidst the sacred memories, poems and stories in Woven, *Joel holds a mirror for us to fall into. A mirror allowing us to see our own story amidst his own. A mirror that reflects the path we might tread, or indeed the footsteps we have left behind. We have always known Joel's poems offered a whisper of a deeper cacophony of truth and love and hurt and hope –* Woven *is that epoch we have longed to hear.*

Bradon French
Youth Ministry Director, Uniting Church in Australia – Victoria and Tasmania

This is the story of a fish and the vastness of a sea beyond the bowl she has known, a boy and a boat beyond what he could have imagined, and an invitation to the weaving that integrates, liberates and redeems by grace. This is the story of my friend Joel. This is an invitation to a story beyond fundamentalism, cynicism and bitterness to the beauty of an expansive faith.

Jarrod McKenna
Peace award-winning Activist, Educator, Pastor; Founding Director, CommonGrace.org.au; Co-host, *In-Verse* podcast

The current global context often presents as a battle ... of conservative fundamentalism and liberal fundamentalism ... Joel's book, Woven, *seeks to ask, 'Is there a way to grab the pendulum that seems to swing wildly between these two extremes, and rock it more gently through the middle? Is there a way to shape the conversation of human dignity and spirituality that does not resort to these and other destructive labels?'*

Terry LeBlanc
Founding Chair and Director, North American Institute for Indigenous Theological Studies; Executive Director, Indigenous Pathways

A Faith
for the Dissatisfied

JOEL McKERROW

ACORN PRESS

Published by Acorn Press
An imprint of Bible Society Australia
ACN 148 058 306
GPO Box 4161
Sydney NSW 2001
Australia
www.acornpress.net.au | www.biblesociety.org.au

ISBN: 978-0-647-53032-0 (pbk); 978-0-647-53033-7.

A catalogue record for this
book is available from the
National Library of Australia

NATIONAL
LIBRARY
OF AUSTRALIA

Editor: Owen Salter.

Cover concept: James de Vries.

Typesetting: John Healy.

Dedicated to
my wife and two children.

You, dear family,
sustain me.

Thank you.

Contents

Foreword

More than a half century ago Thomas Merton said: 'The problem today is that there are no deserts, only dude ranches.' I recently read an essay from Wendell Berry wherein he said: 'A stand consisting only of the best trees would be a tree farm, not a forest.' We live in a time of dude ranches and tree farms equipped with telephone wires and dumpsters. We are not a death and life, light and dark, old and new, trees-we-love and trees-we-could-do-without sort of society. By most accounts, we are about as wild as a small lapdog with a stick in its mouth. Most of us have never lived long enough in a desert to be so hungry and thirsty that we find ourselves chasing down what looks like an oasis, only to disappointedly discover that, all along, it was merely a mirage. And most of us haven't spent enough time working in a forest to understand the value of letting the dead, fallen trees lie with the new living ones, and all of the positive benefits this can have on the soil.

I was recently shown a picture of the Shalom Wildlife Zoo located just 15 miles from our home here in Wisconsin. They have built an exhibit there consisting of two giant windows to look through. One of the windows provides a perfectly unobstructed view of nature at its finest. Above this window are the words 'Window to Wisdom.' The other window's view is obstructed with pasted cut-outs of entertainment news organisations along with names of higher-level education and learning organisations. Above this window are the words 'Window to Knowledge.' The point is: humanity is in trouble, not for lack of knowledge, but for lack of experiential wisdom. Our ability to see clearly has often been limited rather than enhanced by our access to information.

The problem with dude ranches and tree farms is that we get to control the experience. If we want to grow in wisdom, we must first realise that wisdom is wild. That wisdom can only be gained by living in wild places where opposites collide and coexist. We grow in wisdom when our lives are wild enough to go hungry. We grow in wisdom when the lights have been turned out on us and electricity alone can't get them turned back on.

We live in a time of dualism. A time of fences and walls. And should we ever be tempted to think that Donald Trump is the only one building them, think again. For we are an us vs them, fat vs skinny, rich vs poor, less vs more culture. The remedy to dualism is distinction, but we have very few places where distinctions are celebrated, much less *woven* together into a beautiful tapestry for us to see and experience. We have been programmed to build Judgemental Societies rather than Sacramental Societies. The dualism keeps us separated. Distinction has the ability to hold us together and make us whole if we have the courage for it, but growing in that kind of courage will take time, experience and discipline. In *Woven*, Joel McKerrow highlights this sort of experience by telling us his own story of being a white, clean-cut, red-haired religious kid from an upper-class area of Australia who finds himself washing dishes at a shelter with a street worker (a prostitute) and suddenly realising that she has a name, and lines around her face, and a story, and a context. He realises that she is human, and that the cultural space between them has had a falsely de-humanising effect on the other. By serving together, these dividing walls have been forced to come down, and now they are washing dishes together and being given the opportunity to see each other through an unobstructed window for the very first time.

After decades of very popular deconstruction movements, we are still left with very little vision for a new creation. Most of these deconstruction movements have amounted to little more than just exchanging one form of narrow-minded dualistic fundamentalism for another. For the most part, these movements really should be called destruction movements, for wise deconstructionists always keep their eyes on the vision of the new creation, realising that 'making all things new' is not about getting rid of all things old. As my friend Brian Zahnd told me on a rainy afternoon in Belfast, after asking him what he thought of the deconstruction movement: 'Jason, we can't deconstruct forever, eventually we have to build something. And we can't restore Art with dynamite.'

I was introduced to Joel McKerrow by a mutual friend in March of 2018. His poetic language and love for Jesus and others slows me down and helps me see. For all of us who are hungry and thirsty, lost in a wilderness, tired of the noises that always want something from us, and unsatisfied by easy answers on life, poverty, race, gender, and inequality, *Woven* is medicine.

Jason Upton
Singer/Songwriter

The Invitation

The human heart is inhabited by many different longings. In its own voice each one calls to your life. Some are easily recognised and the direction to which they call you is clear. Other voices are more difficult to decipher ... Beneath all these is a longing that has somehow always been there and will continue to accompany every future moment of your life ... the voice of the eternal longing within you.

John O'Donohue[1]

The grave

Digging a grave is never an easy task. Never a walk in the park, nor hands held in soft moonlight. It is, rather, a backbreaking task, a sweat-in-the-eye task. Actually, I am not even sure it should be called a 'task'. That word is too easy, too everyday. It should be called a toil. A grindstone. A splinter. A sorrow. It should be called a confrontation. A deliberation. A disturbance. It should be called a cocoon – the moment when nothing can ever remain the same.

The first and only time I have dug a grave was at a small orphanage on the border of Thailand and Burma. A childless mother stood beside me weeping, her sorrow spilling out on the ground. She had left her home in the Burmese mountains days earlier carrying her sick baby on her back. There was no one around to provide the medical attention her boy needed so she had trekked to the Thailand border. She had heard of a lady who took in the sick and displaced from the war in Burma – the same lady who ran the orphanage I had come to visit, The Bamboo School.

She made the long trek.

Her baby did not.

She arrived just as I arrived. She arrived just as her baby died. He must have passed away only a short distance back along the track. I often wonder whether she crossed the border with him still alive or whether

1

he died in his homeland. I am not sure why this question sticks in my mind or if it really matters. A sorrow indeed. A wailing. A moment of great sadness like the many moments of great sadness for those fleeing war around the world.

The Bamboo School, as it is affectionately named, was set up by a New Zealand lady, Momo Cat, as a home for the many children who managed to escape across the border out of Burma and into Thailand. They sought refuge there. They gained an education there. The sick were treated there. Sadly, this was all too late for this baby boy.

As soon as the group of Australians I was with arrived, our bags were dropped at the bamboo huts in which we would be living. Two of us then joined two of the orphan boys in a walk along a road and up through a winding snake path in the hot jungle. Our short hike was accompanied by the sweat-wet, sticky heat that only tropical places can provide. We came out into a clearing. A small gathering of graves lay under the canopy of the bamboo jungle. Bamboo crosses stood barely affixed and falling down, scattered around the clearing. They marked more moments of loss for people I would never meet. They stood like soldiers guarding their fallen friends. Soldiers badly withered in the heat of the Burmese jungle.

A spare section of the land was chosen by the two boys and then came the hard work. With sweat dripping from our bodies, we took to the ground. Shovels and picks and splinters. At first the earth refused us. It did not want to receive a boy taken so soon. We scratched at the hard surface until, finally, it seemed to let up and allowed the grave to be dug. A hole slowly emerged, large enough to fit the small white casket that now carried the baby boy.

I do not remember his name, or his face covered with a cloth, white and crocheted. I do remember the face of his mother. Streaked in tears dripping to the ground. She stood surrounded by strangers at the burial of her baby boy.

Never have I lost as this mother had lost. Never have I had to let go so thoroughly. I cannot imagine the pain. She wore heartache around her shoulders, sorrow closer than skin. Garments that she would not remove for the rest of her days.

2

I picked up one corner of the casket. Bleached white, golden hinges, heavy. Not heavy enough. We lowered life into death, the rectangular casket filling the hole just dug. Too soon. She took the first lump of churned earth and scattered it down upon the white, upon the boy cut from her body. The gathered children sang a Burmese song, and we all sang *Amazing Grace*. I doubted it at the time.

~

While my own experience on that day couldn't even begin to compare to the grief that this mother knew, while I did not feel the weight of such sorrow, I had my own confrontation in that moment, my own disturbance, my own grindstone.

The unfairness of it all heaped upon me: the anger at injustice and my own laziness, the exasperation at a God who could have prevented this, the sheer frustration at a world that favours those with money and those born in certain countries. The self-loathing that I too was such a person. I wanted to vomit. The safe, comfortable and privileged world I knew back home in Australia cracked under the weight of all this sorrow. Each shovel-load thrown upon the casket was burdened down heavy with dirt and all that was wrong with our world. The questions began to pile on top of each other, all Jenga and ready to tumble.

Why was I not told about this reality? Or was I told and just chose to ignore it all? Why does God let this happen? How could I believe in a God who claimed to be love? How could I live so comfortably and this boy couldn't even get medicine? Didn't God have a plan for this boy's life too? What did my Christianity have to say to this? How could I now live life the same?

Standing beside the grave, I stretched myself out into the ache, into the questions that arose. I demanded an answer from the God I followed. No answer came. There was no easy solution. No voice from the heavens. Just the sound of a crack. The feel of a tear. A rip. The world that I knew splitting at its seams.

It leaves me stunned how one moment can change everything. The entire trajectory of my life instantly U-turned. I wonder now at the serendipity of it all. Serendipity. It was Horace Walpole who coined the term. In a letter from 1754 he describes the word as being taken from a fairy tale called 'The Three Princes of Serendip', and writes that the princes were 'always making discoveries, by accidents and sagacity, of things they were not in quest of.'[2] Finding that which we were never searching for. The unexpected. Perhaps this is the truest point of all learning and growth.

So it was that one question chased after another, each question spurring one more. My head span from their chaos. This grave was a contradiction with no easy solution. A question with no answer. It reminded me of how small I truly am. How much I do not know. How far I have to go. My privileged and comfortable reality peeled back for me to see the world as it truly is. This moment was a cocoon, a spiritual awakening in the shape of a grave. It was questions that began a quest. It was an invitation of serendipity – to stumble upon that which I did not realise I was missing.

There must be more than this

Months later and I am back home in Australia, and I simply can't put things back together. The trip had taken me from Thailand to the Sudan and then Uganda. From seeing one traumatic reality to the next. From witnessing utter despair in poverty, and utter joy in it too. It shattered my perspective. The questions kept coming. The dissatisfaction kept hurting. It was the realising that I had been living for so long ignorant of the world around me, the knowing that there had to be a better way to live.

Yet at the same time came the voices drawing me back to the comfort of the answers I was so used to. The cliché of easy statements. The bliss of ignorance. How tempting to run from dark jungles and Burmese graves into well-trodden pathways. How easy to fall back into lethargy, to let the uncomfortable slide off and away and to embrace all the Western Dream had to offer. I felt the fear of changing my life. But I also felt some kind of liberation. Indeed, what was opening up inside me was both a fear and a freedom. A hope lay down next to the sorrow of that experience in Burma. It had been a grave, but also a cocoon – the tearing

4

down of a world too small and the whispering call of something larger. The offer of a new way to be in this world. It was a painful crack in the facade of my life and it was the stretch of sunlight creeping through its yielding. One hand anxious and clenched, the other hoping and open. It was a widening-field feeling, a walking out from the small pathways of surety. A submitting to a broader space and a beckoning graciousness. And an ache – always the ache.

There must be more than this.

There must be more than the world I had known. The faith I had grown up in. The life I had lived. And the God I believed in. It was a whisper that persisted, a dissatisfaction constant in my life for many years. I did not realise the string I had just pulled. I did not realise how one thread can unravel everything.

I heard all around me the familiar voices that beckoned me to remain in safety, to stay in the security of the shallow end of the pool. They told me not to ask those questions that don't have answers. Especially about God. Especially about the church. And especially about poverty and race and gender and inequality. Do not stir the pot. Swallow down the dissatisfaction. Get on with the way things have always been.

But the ache wouldn't leave.

There must be more than this.

How time slows when you are on the precipice, between the shallows and the strong current of the deep river. The ground feels slippery beneath your feet. Voices battle for your attention. A look back reveals the smiling, unsure faces of dear loved ones, concerned parents, troubled pastors and anxious friends. A look forward reveals only the unknown, the mystery, the precipice where the questions battle it out with the answers. The tug of the tide, the pull of the river, the dark night, the split of light at the dawn, the confrontation, the deliberation, the opening of a cocoon, the whisper of the wind through the open field, the beckoning, the ache, the invitation. The knowing that there must be more.

The invitation. Do you feel it?

What would your yearning say if you let it speak?

There must be more than this.

It comes sometimes as an itch. Sometimes as a frustration. Sometimes an anger. Sometimes unspeakable joy. Sometimes a mystical moment. Sometimes a truth. Sometimes a question. Sometimes a crumbling. Sometimes an opening. Sometimes a grave. Sometimes a rebirth. Sometimes it comes simply as pain and brokenness. However it comes, it comes regardless, to each and every one of us. It comes and it beckons us forward – if we choose to listen.

This book is an invitation. An invitation to meet yourself.

Who would you meet if one day you turned a corner and happened to come across yourself?

Would you like that person? Would you even recognise that person?

Someone once asked, 'Is it possible that you can live your whole life and never meet the person who is living your life?'

There are two things that you can be certain of as you read this book. You are stuck in the present and you are stuck with yourself. Your whole self. No matter how busy you have become, no matter how far you attempt to run, no matter how *spiritual* you are, no matter how *perfect* you strive to be. *You* will always be there keeping yourself company.

Therefore, a radical acceptance of who you are now is the only way to bring about a movement forward in your life. Change always occurs in the present. The invitation is for now. The past is settled, it cannot be changed. The future is fiction, it has not yet come to pass. The only thing that you have the ability to change is *now*. The moment between the past and the future. This is the only moment you have access to. It is your stepping stone. For when you change in the present, you also change the way you view the past, and consequently the way you approach the future. Change is a thousand steps, a million moments. Each of these steps is what is happening in the now, who you are in the present, warts and doubts and screw-ups and all.

So we start by slowing down. We start by seeking to understand who we have become in the here and now, in the deep places. We start by meeting ourselves again.

The invitation of this book is to put on the brakes and let go of progress and pursuit. To allow yourself to be where you are at, right now. Both good and bad. To attempt a few moments of being present and listening, of not having to prove yourself or your worth. This is not a book for those who have it all together. It is a book for the stumbling and the bumbling, the lost, the wandering, the fractured, the doubtful, the hurt. Please do not stop reading, though, if you feel your life is complete and content. May you, who think you have things *figured out*, put aside your *knowing*, just for a moment, and come open-handed towards possibility and redirection.

This is a book for those who call themselves religious and those who do not. It is for the spiritually enlightened, for those who dance in the river, and for those whose river bed dried up to dust a long time ago. It is for the passionate, for the yearning, for those whose fires burn bright, for the hopeful. It is for the weary, the burnt-out, the wandering, the aimless, the doubtful.

This book is an open table. It is open for any and all to come and take their place in its discourse. Christian, atheist, Buddhist, Muslim. Gay, straight, transgender. Conservative, progressive, liberal. Powering on in your spirituality or exiled from your own inner landscapes. Passionate or barely crawling. Whoever you are, you are welcome here. All of you – not just the nice parts, but all the parts. The broken parts, the shamed parts, the guilty parts, the angry parts, the hurt parts, the desperate parts. Come, find shelter. This book is a shelter.

May you find safety for your soul in the circumference of these words. Not as a boundary around you, but as a nest to hold you, gently. A soft and tender grace. May these words be as unassuming and yet as constant as the tides. May the sea of these questions rub up against the land of your knowing. May you learn to yield as the shoreline of your soul gives itself to be carved by the wild waves. The artistry of the tides will shape you into something new and true and beautiful. This book is an ocean tide.

Indeed, I have come to realise that Jesus is the same. An ocean tide. Washing away. Shaping the new and the true and the beautiful. This book is about Jesus. It is about my journey toward Jesus. Which may sound strange to some of you, but it is true. It is a journey of losing a Jesus that was too small and looked way too much like me, to a Jesus that began to mesmerise me. A Jesus calling me to something much grander and more holistic and more inclusive than I had thought possible. A Jesus who was drawing me into the true and into the beautiful.

The response

That is what lies at the heart of my desire for you as you read this book: *formation into the true and the beautiful*. Even in the pages that make you uncomfortable. I only name the bleak and the unpleasant because by naming their reality we may then begin to see them transformed. This is my hope. I am filled with hope. Hope in who we are now. Hope in who we are becoming.

As you read, there will inevitably be times when you are impacted with either a felt emotional response or a strong stance for or against the concepts I explore. There will be times when your buttons are pushed, and out of you arises a feeling of either resonance or resistance. Resonance and resistance – that which we are attracted to and that which repels us. Those things that ignite a fire and those that throw water on the fire. Those things we love and those we fear.

Both of these are absolutely valid feelings. They are emotions entangled with thoughts that are telling you something about your perspective, about the things you hold dear.

The challenge I put before you is not to allow yourself to be dictated to by these feelings. Please do not erect walls of defence, either when resistance is felt or through being overjoyed that your own beliefs are being affirmed when resonance occurs. Neither of these moves us forward. Often what they do is stop us from truly hearing what the other is saying. We think we know what someone is talking about because we hear certain words or phrases (words like 'evangelical' or 'white privilege' or 'pro-choice') and immediately place these into our predetermined judgements. All I ask is for you not to build up your defence and rebuttals when resistance comes.

This is not so I may convince you that my understanding is the way things are meant to be. This book is not an attempt to convert you to my views or tell you that your own spirituality, if it be different from mine, is not valid. This is not an attempt to place your experiences below mine or to negate what has been in your life.

And I ask for the same courtesy: that you read this book loosely. That you not feel you have to shout down where I am coming from when it differs from your own perspective. Perhaps it is OK to listen to difference. May you acknowledge the resonance and resistance, and instead of allowing them to dictate, ask yourself why they may have arisen when they did. Why did this thought come to mind? What is it rubbing up against within you? What buttons were pressed, and why are these particular buttons important to you?

The three

I have split this book into three phases, three movements, three postures of the self, as it were.

The Sculpted Self.
The Unravelled Self.
The Woven Self.

Three phases of the journey.

Where we begin.
The path we walk.
The place we come to.

The place we begin. The Sculpted Self. This is where our spirituality, our way of seeing and being in the world, is shaped and socialised by the nurturing community around us.

The path we walk. The Unravelled Self. This is when our socialised, sculpted absolutes crumble into questions and doubts and deconstruction and critique.

The place we come to. The Woven Self. This is where we come to the far end of the desert of our deconstruction and our life and world find a reconstruction, a new weave, a new way of being, a new way of seeing and a new way of doing. Here the inside and the outside are held together.

Before we begin to understand these three movements, however, it must be acknowledged that one cannot really make such a distinct progressional split in the realities of life and things of spiritual growth. From sculpted, to unravelled, to woven – no journey is ever this linear.

No person's existence can be reduced to the quantifiable, especially when it comes to the spiritual realities of life. We do not start at stage one, move everything over to stage two and then out into stage three. Life does not work like this.

We will always be moving back and forth in various ways, at various times, in and out of these postures. Some areas of thought and life and faith and self will always remain sculpted. Perhaps there are some parts of us that need this solidity. Other areas will crumble and may never find their right place in the world. Other areas still may find their reconstruction, their weave into a whole, only to be shaken loose once more.

Life is complex and humanity is complex. Movement is always messy. But, for the sake of the way we take in information, it is easier to process in the form of stages or phases. So though it may not be as distinct and sequential in life, the splitting into three in this book gives us a way to enter in. To understand the generalised movements of the spiritual journey.

Rather than seeing these as linear, sequential, distinct stages, it is far better to understand them as modes of being built one on top of the other and entangled together. An ever-deepening circle rather than a linear progression. The out-workings of this look very different for each person and their specific journey. It is not cookie-cut spirituality I am speaking of here; it is not programable spiritual growth. We do not move out of one into the next, throwing out the old and giving our whole selves to the new. We take who we are in the first phase and build onto that the realities of the next, and so on. It is back and forth, to and fro. The spiritual journey is one mode building on the other while at the same time subverting and challenging what it is building on. Deconstruction and reconstruction lie side-by-side, until, by their circling, we are slowly and gradually remade.

Three movements.
Three phases.
Three building blocks.
Three postures of spirituality.
Three modes of being.
The sculpted.

The unravelled.

The woven.

This book is a question. It holds within it no clear cut and easy cliché. It is no self-help manual describing the seven steps to spiritual fulfilment. Any such thing will only leave us more trapped. This is a book about the journey. It is not a book of answers – the journey rarely is – and it is not a book about what you need to know. It is a book about how you come to know what you already know, and how you might be able to see beyond the frame through which you have always viewed the world.

This is a book of story. It is my own story. There is no other story I can write. I write from my own experience, my own history, my own sculpting tradition, my own unravelling, my own seeking to find a weave. I write from a place of humility. I do not have the answers, just the observations and the wonderings.

So take time as you read to pause and reflect, and to ask the questions that are stirring. Bring your own life into the context of these reflections and see what emerges. Bring your doubts and frustrations and struggles and questions and sit in the invitation.

The invitation is to the grindstone

> to the splinter
> to the confrontation
> to enter the cocoon
> to the moment where nothing can ever remain the same again.

The invitation is a beckoning towards movement

> towards allowing your world to be shaken
> towards seeing things differently.

The invitation is a movement into hope.

Part 1:
The Sculpted Self

A Boat Story

The boy was given a boat. A wooden boat. A small boat for a small boy. The perfect fit. He could reach the oars and the tiller and the ropes all from where he sat.

His father made him the boat, and each day he would look on from the nearby shore telling his son what to do. How to paddle. How to hoist the sail. How to tie the knots. The boy learned it all, and so began to manoeuvre around the harbour by himself.

Occasionally the wind would pick up and the waves would rock the boat, and the boy would be scared. But he knew that the harbour walls would protect him, and his dad was near enough to rescue him. So he kept on sailing. Every day. Around and around that little harbour.

He learned every part of it. Memorised the rocks and the sand dunes and where the coral rose up beneath the water, and where the rip could take you out of the mouth of the harbour and out to sea. And he knew all the boats tied up to the docks. Those old and falling apart that hadn't left the harbour since he was born. Those that would go out and not return for days or weeks or months. Those that never came back.

The boy wondered what was out there. He would stare at the horizon beyond the harbour wall and something would swell inside. But his dad would call out and warn him not to stray too near the mouth of the breakwater wall.

So he would turn back and continue his sailing.
Around and around and around.

Sculpted

We live on an island surrounded by a sea of ignorance. As our island of knowledge grows, so does the shore of our ignorance.

John Archibald Wheeler[3]

Side-by-side

Chipped purple fingernails sank slowly into tepid water. Glistening soap suds. Fingers that scrubbed away the food. They mingled there, her fingers, washed clean with the saucers and the cups.

'The years don't clean away so easily now, do they?'

Her comment floated out into the space between us. We were standing side-by-side washing dishes at the kitchen sink of a drop-in centre for street workers. Side-by-side. The good Christian boy and the street worker. Side-by-side. Before this day, she didn't have a name. She was just a prostitute. She lived in a world that may as well have belonged on another planet. Side-by-side. My sheltered teenage existence and her fight-to-survive reality. Side-by-side.

Among my schoolmates she would have been called 'the whore on the corner'. Such are the harsh judgements we make of what we do not understand. They are always born of our ignorance.

Ignorant. We were certainly that.

I smiled awkwardly at her poignant half-joke. Her flaking nail polish speckled purple on the white soap suds. She passed me the plates and I wrapped a towel around each one. My hands shook slightly. I was nervous and I was not sure why.

As she gave me the cutlery, I stole a quick glance at the side of her face. Studied the lines. Lost myself wondering at the stories they held. Ever inquisitive, I was hooked on the stories that lay behind people's faces. She turned her head slightly towards me and I looked away, hoping she hadn't seen me staring.

15

This was the first day I had ever spent time with a street worker. It had been an awkward lunchtime meal. This was her place, not mine. I had come to her territory, her neighbourhood, her street, her corner. A world I had gladly not been a part of, until now. Side-by-side. I felt as out of place as I am sure I looked. Straight-laced, clean-cut, short red hair, button-down shirt boy, standing next to short skirt, torn leggings, thick make-up, ageing lady from the corner. Side-by-side.

As I dried dishes, I remembered how not that long before I had come down this same street in a car with my mates. All laughing and joking and calling out names at the girls on the street. Perhaps at this very lady I was now washing dishes with. I had mocked and I had laughed.

I just did not realise they were human – the girls, that is. Not my mates; their humanity is still debatable.

I did not realise they were human, so I treated them as foreign, as alien, as something other than human. It was easier that way. To either ignore or dehumanise. Had I given any sense of credence to their reality, their story, it would have resulted in questions for myself too hard to answer. Instead I cast them in the harsh light of judgement and saw them as something less. I chose to ignore, to mock, to erect a wall and declare them outside. A fence to hide behind.

Walls and fences. I have built many during my life. To keep uncomfortable people out. To keep unfamiliar ideas out. To stay safe inside.

But I must tell you, I have come to dislike fences.

The first fence I ever hated was the electric fence that I peed on as a child. It was not a fun day. There are, after all, only two types of people in this world: those who learn from the others who go before them and those who just have to go and pee on the fence themselves. I was always the latter.

The second fence I came to hate was when I was a teenager, a few years before grave digging and standing side-by-side at the kitchen sink. It was a corrugated-iron fence that stood tall behind my hotel in Vanuatu. A boy's face peeked over the top and I wondered who he was. So I walked from hotel room past swimming pool and across lush green grass and stood on tiptoe to glance over the fence.

There I saw a boy and his sister. They stood knee-high in rubbish and the scrimmage of desperation.

I leaned on the fence. It was a demarcation – where manicured green abruptly stopped and the dirt of an ugly city began. A separation of two worlds. The grass is never greener on the other side when we keep all the water to ourselves. I wanted to tear the fence down. I was not yet brave enough in myself to even call out to them. My life was so far removed from theirs. I was scared of their difference, their desperation. The flimsy corrugated-iron fence was suddenly impassable, and I turned back to the hotel.

This was where my dislike of fences began. The walls that divide us. Corrugated iron or white picket palings. They both separate us. Built high to keep them out, to hold us in. Yet 'holding' is not the right word. Fences do not hold us; they scare us into rigidity, into security, into a small space.

I have stood on the Palestinian side of the border and placed hands like a prayer on the mortar where a boy showed me Banksy, but he could not show me his girlfriend because she lived on the other side of the wall. A fence he was not allowed to cross. I have walked in Berlin by the wall that was torn down. Twenty-five years of separation of mother from daughter, father from son. I have kneeled in Dachau prison camp, hands torn by the barbed wire of genocide. I have stood in Belfast at the Peace Wall. I do not know why we would ever call it a 'peace wall'. No wall has ever been about peace.

Sorry, Mr Trump, but I have never liked walls or fences. I do not like their demarcation and their prejudice. Yet though I may not like them, I have let myself be trapped by them again and again. Many times, closed. Many times, secure. Many times, scared. And most often without realising it.

And then there are the fences we can't see. Glass fences. Transparent fences. Fences that surround us though we do not even recognise them. We swim inside their holding like little fishes in glass bowls. Swimming around in circles.

Little fishes, every one of us

My favourite saying ever is this: *A fish in a bowl doesn't know it is wet.*

It has been surrounded by its water environment for as long as it has been a fish. Swimming around and around, blind to the way the water shapes its reality. It has not known the existence of dryness, so how could it know its own wetness? The water is both its habitat and its master. The entirety of its world.

I too have swum in many fishbowls throughout my lifetime. Swimming circles within glass walls. The fishbowls of family, school, media, church, whiteness, middle-class culture, friends, masculinity. All fishbowls. All filled with water that immersed me, infilled me and entrapped me. The glass walls held the substance of my life. How could I know there was anything different?

Until I looked over a hotel fence in Vanuatu.

Until I dug a grave for a boy in Burma.

Until I stood side-by-side with her, button shirt next to too-short skirt.

This lady did not belong in my fishbowl. I did not belong in hers. Yet I owe her everything. She showed me my reality. Her very existence was a mirror to the world I knew, pointing out the circles I swam in.

Little fishes, every one of us.

We have all swum in circles. We have all grown up not realising the wetness of the water. Familiarity is a curse not easily broken. And are we not all shaped, from our birth, in worlds not of our own making? Be you a straight-laced church kid or a lady on the street. The fishbowl is inevitable and inescapable.

Indeed, this is how it was meant to be. Growth always happens in a social context. We are shaped in a specific way by those around us. We are fashioned to be like them. They are the pattern of how we too should be in the world. Our fishbowls are crucial to our existence and the development of our identity.

A sandcastle

Now, pick up the fishbowl. Fill it with sand, down by the beach. Turn it over and make a sandcastle.

Picture it: a sandcastle on a beach on a rainy day.

Each drop of rain falls down to meet the sandcastle. The sand, though, does not stand in defiance and unmoved. The sand does not resist like concrete. It receives the droplets of rain and in turn is affected by them. With each drop of water from the sky, small indentations are made on the top of the sandcastle. The heavier the rain, the larger these indentations become. The water droplets begin to spill out over the edge. They form small rivulets trickling down the castle walls. It is pouring now. The rain on the top of the sandcastle creates ever-deepening craters. Deeper and more defined, the rivulets become channels of water flowing down the side of the castle and out to the sea. Any droplet that falls on the sandcastle cannot help but flow down one of these side gutters. The sandcastle is streaked with channels of water, carved by its water sculptor. It receives the water and is shaped by it.

The brain too is a sandcastle. It does not resist the rain of the senses. From birth it receives raindrops of sensory information that it then channels into rivulets. Neurologists call them 'neural pathways'. They say the brain is made up of billions of interconnecting neurons that receive information from the craters created by the senses and let this water flow down the interpretive channels of their sandcastle walls. We receive and interpret this input according to what has already been shaped by the rains of our past. Through the hard rainfall of repetition, these water channels, these neural pathways, become engrained within us. This is the only way we can function in the world. We know what to do when our stomach starts telling us we are hungry because our brains have been patterned this way.

When you read the name 'Donald Trump', the input through your eyes flows as electrical signals along one of the millions of neural pathways your brain has created to interpret your reality. Your brain recalls the information it has stored about Donald Trump, and so you have a category by which to understand and respond. Your brain's library recalls a response depending on your past experience and upbringing. If you are a patriotic American Republican, if you are socially progressive, if you are a woman, if you are a man, if you are black, if you are white, if you are a young Muslim boy growing up in Iraq or Afghanistan – whoever you are, your response to the name 'Donald Trump' will be decidedly different according to the conditioning your brain has gone through.

The same applies to the names Jesus or Buddha or Mohammad. Or the word 'atheist'. All of these terms are understood by you through this neural patterning, the way your brain has been wired by your past experience.

This has huge implications for our spirituality.

The greatest of these may be the simple reality that we can never think freely of our own accord. We always interpret the world around us by our past. We are always shaped and moulded by the rain of experience, by the words we have heard, by the actions we have seen and felt. Forever biased, we can only ever interpret the world through our neural pathways. We see the world through painted lenses – lenses that have been coated by family, by society, by church, by tradition, by the places we have called home.

These are the realities that sculpt our existence in the world, whether you are a straight-laced church kid or an ageing lady on the street.

The Fishbowl of Home

Family love is messy, clinging, and of an annoying and repetitive
pattern, like bad wallpaper.

Friedrich Nietzsche[4]

The table

Shuffle of feet. Clasp of hands. Palms placed beneath one's butt cheeks
to stop them from stealing food from the table. Dad reads the Bible.
The unanimous sigh of siblings. The dulcet tones of my father. Brothers
kicking shins out of sight beneath the wood. Staring at the steaming
food, all Pavlov and hungry. This was the beginning of many a mealtime
in the McKerrow household.

Before the eating came the listening. Father expounding the
Scriptures. Mother trying to quieten down the kids. Dad reading the
stories of Daniel in the lion's den, of David singing songs, of Moses in
the desert, of Jesus healing lepers. From the stories came the morals, and
from the text came the doctrines, and from both came the values. That
which we would shape our lives around. Our religion.

The Bible was closed. We held hands. A sacred ring of family prayer.
One of us was chosen to say grace, and the words of thanks tumbled
out fast and incoherent in the haste of hungry children blurting out a
prayer so they could get to the eating. An older brother's grip purposely
tightened. My fingers turned purple and I tried not to yell in pain, instead
letting my head fall to the wooden table and blocking out the agony. The
sloppy unison of 'Amen'. A sacred ring indeed. Waiting. Salivating. Forks
lifted. Mouths opened. Meatloaf downed in seconds.

This was the table where the McKerrow family ate and fought and
laughed and learned and prayed and grew and talked. The table was the
pulpit of my father. Dad's sermons echoed down the corridors of eager
minds. It was the table where we broke bread and spoke of things sacred.
Where we were taught the way the world works, taught the rules and

21

taught the doctrines. This was where we were taught life.

At the table we were told the name of God.
At the table we were baptised in his love.
At the table Dad was never wrong. That table was built damn strong.

The table was the great educator. It was our place of formation. Our fishbowl. Our sculptor. And how thankful I am for it. It created a structure for how the McKerrow children would engage with the world. It gave us a framework to hang our life experience on. It gave us a container to fit our worlds within.

We needed that table. We needed some way to compute life, to grasp it and not let it overwhelm. We needed some way to understand life's haphazard events. We needed the rules, though we hated them at the time. We needed the doctrines. They were the solid structure we built our life and faith on, the base foundation of our certainties. We needed a belief system. We needed a strong moral code.

We needed a table.
We needed to be sculpted.
We needed it all.

Though we did not realise it then, the table could only ever take us so far.

~

Every single person has grown up around a kitchen table, or a breakfast bar, or a sofa in front of the TV, or a fireplace. The family home, its love and its neglect. We are painted by it. Bright colours of happy memory. A coating of grey and loss. Some tables religiously conservative. Others filled with ambivalence and anger towards all things religious and spiritual. Around the kitchen table some have known a deep care and concern for who they are and their becoming in this world. Others have known only fear born of harsh scorn, the hurt of being misunderstood and a sense of abandonment they are never quite able to shake.

We were shaped around tables of loud debate, tables of silence, tables of quick temper, tables shaking with laughter, tables aglow with television rays, tables of great freedom, tables that demanded adherence to strict rules and even harsher consequences. You are what you eat, they say. We take on the shape of our tables.

These tables are why most Christian young people are people who have grown up in Christian households upholding Christian beliefs, and why most Muslim young people are people who have grown up in Muslim households upholding Islamic beliefs. The same goes for atheists, for right-wing conservatives, for left-wing alternatives – for whatever persuasion about whatever reality in life. We all begin with an inherited understanding of the world.

It was around the table that we all became religious. Yes, *all of us.*

Whether explicitly or implicitly, we inherited a worldview, a moral framework, an ethical foundation, a way of relating, a faith system. We took on deep convictions about the make-up of the world and learned how these convictions would play out in our ritualistic actions – be they the actions of attending church or attending the shopping mall or attending the football game. These became our religious appropriations, the things we deem sacred and are devoted to. All of us are religious even if we have never stepped into a church or a mosque.

It was around the table that we were all taught of life and love and God and self and the kindness and cruelty of relationship. It was around the table that a future was mapped out for us. The rest of our lives have then been shaped both by the table and by our very rebellion against it. Either way, our life is mapped around what came before us.

When anyone turns their gaze inward, to discover the deeper parts of the self and how these parts echo out into their life, it is inevitable that they are led back to both the generosity and the poverty of the family home.

An inheritance

The family home is the first crucible of our existence. Walls built around sharp angles of expectation. A roof that both shelters and over-protects. The attic of our secrets. The bathroom of privacy. The basement of our shame. The laundry where we find ourselves clean once more. The loungeroom of relationship. The fireplace, a hearth to hold us together. The front yard, a doorway to somewhere other, an invitation. The backyard, a gateway to adventure, a beckoning.

Behind the house, through the backyard, runs a river. It flows down from our ancestors – their life that shaped the life of their children, and their children, and their children, and streaming now into our self-dwelling. We are birthed not just from parents but from a long line of people. The family home is painted with their stories, layered thick on the walls, whether we can see them or not. They are a river running deep through our self-landscape. Their story birthed a story, which birthed a story, which birthed a story, which birthed you. You are a confluence of the many stories, the many lifetimes that stretch out behind you. The rivers that now come together to show you that you are not just you but the continuation of them. The intertwining of real life and family fable all gathered together around the family table.

An inheritance is often seen as the estate left to us when these ancestors pass. Land. Money. Possessions. A will that is written. But there is a will that is unwritten. It is our inevitable inheritance, much deeper than possessions. Fables etched into tables to tell you who to be in this world.

What was your family table like?

What were the stories told around it?

What were the stories that were not told around it?

What did you inherit?

Many cannot speak of family without lament; without anger and the fracture of abandonment. The pressure. The feeling of never being enough. The scarring of abuse. So much that is inherited from family can tie a person down. The hurt and the pain. The shaping force you wish was not a shaping force. But it was, and it is. And it can be a knife that you let linger in your back, a poison you let keep poisoning. It can dictate everything else.

Or perhaps it doesn't have to.

I am not saying here that you can just get rid of it or that you won't be shaped by the family fishbowl you have swum in. Your past *will* shape you. But as a friend of mine once said, you do not have to let it dictate your existence in the world. You are shaped, but you are still your own person. You still make your own choices.

My friend's name was 'Jess'. Her growing-up life was filled with abuse and anger. Her father treated her worse than most will ever experience, and he still does. She sent me a text message the other day that she received from him, one that called her the harshest of names – names I would never call anyone. All her life this has been her fishbowl. And yet this incredible woman, this strong mother of many, this creative, this force of nature has one of the biggest hearts I have ever known – compassionate to the core. And all the things she is now is who she has chosen to become. Who she chooses to become every day. Who she fights to be regardless of the fishbowl of her family.

Jess tells me that she is on a journey of forgiveness and that she wants her father to know that she forgives him. And I do not understand this. How could she? But this is her story, and it inspires me and challenges me. Her life has been shaped but not dictated.

Who we are now is the outflow of who we have become in the depth of our being over the many years of circle-swimming inside our fishbowls. We live out of this wellspring. We pour it out into our relationships, our spirituality, our vocation; into how we dress, into how we shop, into everything we touch. It affects all of life, yet we understand it little. We rarely connect our everyday decisions and how we conduct ourselves with the fishbowls we have swum in. We do not realise our own wetness. We live out of an unexamined existence, a socialised worldview. A frame of life we can call *the Sculpted Self*.

~

The Sculpted Self is who we have become through the family we have been sculpted by. It is the way the world was taught to us, the rules given to us. Indeed, it is the part of life that is shaped around external rules and expectations – rules taught by family, by schools, by television, by culture, by the authoritative figures of our social spheres. Rules that tell us what to do, when to do it, when to be where, what to wear, what to eat, what to listen to. These rules are the expectations of the communities we are part of. We need to know them. We need the consistency and the delineation of right/wrong and good/bad.

When my children were first born, they were totally reliant on their mother and me for absolutely everything. Food. Water. Shelter. Warmth. Love. They would have died without our care. As my children are growing, they are becoming less dependent. They are walking forward into the freedom of their lives with an ever-lessening need for us, their parents.

Yet I am not about to give $5 to my four-year-old son, drop him off at the local shops and tell him I'll pick him up in a few hours. A four-year-old cannot handle the freedom of this. When he becomes a teenager, this will change. As a parent, I will be learning to let him go. To let him swim outside our family fishbowl and into the fishbowls of wider friendship circles and the fishbowl of our society.

This movement is petrifying for a parent. But leave the home we all must. In the adolescent years, our social conditioning is transferred more and more from family to peers and to the society around us. This world tells us who we should be in our lives. The fishbowl of family is swapped for the fishbowl of society.

The Fishbowl of Society

A mansion on the hill

I am a white, middle-class, Christian, heterosexual, able-bodied, married man with children.

I wouldn't consider myself a racist. I wouldn't call myself a sexist. I wouldn't call myself an ableist. These are names we give to people who are 'bad'. And I am 'good'. Right? Same as you.

Yet while I may not consider myself to be a racist, sexist, ableist, greedy person, in the reality of the fishbowl of my society, I am part of a system that perpetuates inequality between the races, the sexes, those who have and those who have not. I am not only part of it, I am given advantage because of who I am in the system. The failure to acknowledge this is what we may call 'entitlement'.

A privilege is bestowed on me simply because of my skin colour, gender, religion, sexuality, economic status and so on. And most of the time I do not even realise it. I uphold a system of dominance. I perpetuate inequality. I write this book from a privileged position, high atop a mountain of advantage and affluence. I am the dominant culture.

I wholeheartedly admit that, from this height, the clouds can be blinding.

I eat well – too well. An overfull belly. Food coma. I shower every day. Our house has air-conditioning, soft couches, a new sound system, shelves of books I have collected, clean drinking water, clean toilet water. I know greater conditions of comfort than the kings of old in their castles. Even now I write on a computer that has likely been put together using some form of slave labour. I speak on a phone that is the same. I work jobs where I am paid fairly. I am not looked at with suspicion.

From this mountaintop I may write about our social existence only with a deep sense of humility. A recognition of the bias that comes from my place of privilege.

I have no idea what it is to have to struggle to survive; to go without; to stand on a corner taking tricks; to not know where the next day's food or heat will come from; to fear a policeman every time I walk past one; to tolerate unwanted advances on trains; to look over my shoulder as I walk home; to be told I cannot marry someone I love; to be passed over in job applications; to be forced to do what I do not wish to do.

I cannot speak from the perspective of those who have walked under such heavy burdens.

I may only speak from the perspective of one who has the power in this system. I may only speak from my (relative) mansion on the hill. For this is my existence. My sculpted reality. My societal fishbowl. It has taken me many years to realise the effect of this water I swim in. I was lured by it into 'a slavery that is so attractive, comfortable, and titillating we do not recognise it as slavery.'[6]

We have given ourselves to the gods of this culture. Our societal fishbowl shapes everything, from how we shop to how we pray, from our self-perspective to how we see the world around us.

Consumer culture

In high school it is the cafeteria table and the TV and Facebook and Snapchat and iTunes and Spotify that take precedence over the family fishbowl. Autonomy begins. Experimentation. Trying on and rejecting different identities. Rebellion and discovery.

These acts of defiance towards family and subsequent changes in thought, however, do not stem from a well-thought-out negotiation and critique of familial beliefs. Rather, the young person simply jumps from the family fishbowl into the fishbowl of their friends. It is still a socialisation. It is still a sculpted reality. Most often it is a social conditioning for the sake of social acceptance. As teenagers we are one person at home, another at school, another at church, another at work. We sift personas to find the one that fits. We wear multiple masks and swap them often. We are in search of who we are.

During adolescence, most of us become a confusing mixture of an inherited belief system from family and a socialised belief system from our peer group, all jumbled together in the wider fishbowl of Western consumer society. In this mix we desperately crave to know who we are.

And we do not stop this search at adolescence. As adults we still glean our identity and outlook from the fishbowls of our existence. Those around us still serve as a mirror as to who we should be. We still wear our masks. Indeed, none of us can ever rid ourselves of the shaping forces of our lives. A part of us will always be sculpted.

The question then is the extent to which we give ourselves over to this moulding and give up the core of who we are.

The inherent danger of the Sculpted Self is to become so like those around you, so like your sculpting community, that you lose your own distinctiveness. A bland conformity. A squashing down of difference. A denial that can lead easily to the loss of self-definition and a harsh rejection of anyone who does not fit. We move through life being socialised by one group, then another, then another. Chameleon-like and diffused.

In high school, who is in and who is out is decided in social cliques most often based around subcultures. These subcultures are shaped around dress code, interests, music and other social behaviours – the things deemed 'cool' by each particular social group. Those things are made 'cool' by the many multinational corporations vying for a slice of the market in this teen demographic. The roughly $600 billion-a-year advertising industry[7] tells young people what they should be buying to remain acceptable in the social sphere of their fishbowls.

A rough estimate of the average time spent watching TV by an individual in America is 29 hours a week (four hours a day),[8] which is the equivalent of 13 straight years of a lifespan. For those not watching Netflix, up to 27 percent of airtime is advertisements, which means we could possibly spend three continuous years of our entire life watching TV commercials.

The average American sees over 4000 advertisements every day.[9] From magazines, billboards and the internet to radio, TV, movies and music, we are literally inundated with messages from the media machine of Western culture. We are swimming in its waters without even realising. We are part of a society fully immersed in a way of consuming that affects not just the way we shop but our entire outlook on life. It is so pervasive that the advertising agency Young and Rubicam could state, 'Belief in consumer brands has replaced religious faith as the thing that gives people purpose in life.'[10]

~

> Consumption is collectivist-individualist, nationalist-internationalist, the healer, the entertainer, the lover, the spiritual, the feeder and the consolation. It is the chief rival to God in our culture.
>
> **Alan Storkey**[11]

~

We worship in our shopping mall cathedrals. We listen to the sermons of advertisements. We commune through Facebook. We are not merely being entertained by popular culture; we are being taught by it. Shaped by it. Discipled by it. We are told who we are within it. The media is the mediator of our spiritual journeys, the shaper of our theology and our worldview. It is our modern-day priest.

Now, if you are not a particularly religious person, do not let the term *theology* scare you. Theology is simply the study of the Divine and of the relationship of the Divine to humanity. It is the search for meaning and purpose in relation to whatever or whoever we call God. As Edward de Bary writes, where we find our significance is 'where our god(s) reside.'[12]

To know who we are and why we walk the earth, this is theology. It is about our frame of meaning, our point of reference. Theology is not the preoccupation of trained theologians but the preoccupation of every single person. Every time we reflect on meaning and purpose, we are reflecting on the god(s) we follow. We are being theologians.

Each of us holds strong theological convictions, even if we don't realise it. That which we believe but don't realise we believe is our sculpted, implicit theology. It is our under-the-radar belief. If you look long enough at how someone lives, you see the truth they hold on to bleeding out into their lifestyle.

This sculpted theology is implicit in that it has not been intentionally thought out and wrestled with. Rather, we have been imbued with it by the cultural waters we swim in. Unknowingly, each of us has taken on certain beliefs simply because they have flowed over the gills of our understanding through the years. An absent-minded conditioning. A blender of beliefs into which is thrown ingredients from family and church and peers and MTV and Hollywood and celebrities and magazines and Facebook and school.

Without intentional thought, this implicit theology sadly becomes an 'ad-hoc collection of little self-help techniques that we use to take the edge off our materialistic rat-race lives.'[13]

~

Most teenagers swimming in the fishbowl of Western consumerism do not realise how manipulated they are. It never occurs to them that the brands they wear, the drinks they consume and the music they listen to have come to them not through freedom of choice but through the power of a monstrous advertising industry. Sadly, most adults do not realise this either.

In our adult lives, who is in and who is out is determined much like teenage social realities, only on a more expensive scale. The toys have bigger engines. Now on top of clothes and music come cars and houses and job security. An adherence to an expected lifestyle. A keeping up with the Joneses. A hyper-consumption of goods and experiences. Our lives are shaped around economic prosperity and the threat of exclusion should we not live up to our expected societal input. Such is the pressure to conform within this fishbowl that the average businessperson works 45 hours a week and spends just two hours directly with their family.[14]

In a society that revolves around continued economic growth, it is imperative that people keep on purchasing goods and experiences, and working extremely hard to be able to do so. This is why so much money

31

and energy are poured into getting people to work ever-increasing hours and purchase more and more products, regardless of the wider effect this is having on the environment, the family, our perception of self and our expectations of what life is *meant* to look like.

We have been duped by an economic system always reliant on an ever-demanding rat-race. The media machine is oiled by the fears of the masses. The fear of the father, that he is not providing what a good father should for his family. The fear of the teen, that he or she will be left out and considered uncool. The fear of the mother, that she is missing out on a life of adventure and romance. The fake reality of the bodies and the lifestyles of rock stars and movie stars and Disney princesses and TV personalities becomes the carrot dangling just beyond our grasp. The inducement of our anxiety makes us believe the fake promises of products and experiences that can never fulfil us. It is a disastrous cycle.

These are the empty promises of a shallow system that will do anything for profit. We are no longer sold a car or deodorant or beverage based on its function. Instead, advertisers, in their bid to stand out from each other, tap into those deepest human needs of love, belonging, purpose and self-worth and exploit the anxiety that surrounds them. They tell consumers that they deserve the best while at the same time telling them they are too fat or too ugly, and don't have the right hair, the best gadgets, the coolest clothes.

An interviewer on a televised talk show asked a marketing executive, 'How does one go about starting a marketing campaign to sell hamburgers to kids?' The marketing executive replied, 'Find a point of weakness and lust in every man, woman and child and target that weakness to make them want to buy the product.'[15]

Is it any wonder we have produced a society of mass depression, anxiety, eating disorders, divorce and more? Life simply cannot live up to the fake reality we are promised, and so our anxiety increases, and so does our desperate attempt to do anything we can to bring about the promised lifestyle. The 4000 raindrops of advertising that fall on the sandcastle of our brains every day bring about a very fractured perspective. It is the way this system sculpts us.

This sculpting comes not only through the advertising industry but also through the education we provide for our children. Much research shows that education, both implicitly and explicitly, is increasingly being used as a tool to create economically productive members of society, 'turning teachers into missionaries for capitalism.'[16] The official curriculum upholds the dominant narrative of our societal fishbowl. In other words, our education system grooms a society fixated on the Western Dream, with no thought as to the impact on the rest of global and local culture and environment.

Freedom and the system

Both the rich and the poor are victims of this system. The poor are victims trapped on the underside without access. The rich are victims trapped in the rat-race on the upper decks. One is certainly a much harsher victimisation. But both sides end up losing.

One side is devoured from the outside in, by poverty and starvation and desperation. The other is devoured from the inside out, by the modern pandemics of depression and anxiety, by the promises of our media and social system that always leave us wanting, by the demand for progress, by keeping up with the Joneses, by the Western mentality of power and rivalry and dominance, by the constant striving.

This to say it is a *system*, not a person or a group of people, that perpetuates the social inequalities around us. An economic system has shaped generations into seeking comfort for themselves at the expense of others. The system is to blame, not the people caught up in it.

All people need to be freed from the system.

It does me no good to put blame on those higher up the rungs than myself. It is too easy to take cheap pot shots at the well-to-do for their ignorance when I know that I, too, suffer from the same thing. Change does not come from placing blame but from doing what I can with the life I have been given. It comes from owning my reality as one who oppresses without realising it, owning my reality as one duped by the system.

The world is not the way it is because it just appeared as such. The world of today is the product of a system. The world is engineered. This is why you can have good people who perpetuate oppressive realities – such as those of us who do not adamantly stand against the inhumane imprisonment of innocent people who have done nothing but seek safety from war-torn countries. There is something wrong with such moral silence. But it is not the individual people propagating it who are to be blamed. It is the system we are all stuck in. It is 'the powers that be.'

As Jürgen Moltmann wrote of Martin Luther King Jr, not long after he was assassinated:

> Martin Luther King, Jr., sided with the blacks and the poor. He organized protest movements and strikes. These actions were directed against the white racism and the capitalistic society in his country. But at the same time, he was constantly concerned about the white people, unredeemed and enslaved by their pride and anxiety. He mobilized the marches of the blacks and the poor, not for revenge against the whites but for the redemption of the black and white alike from their mutual estrangement.[17]

A mutual estrangement. A society fractured. How I need those who do not swim in the waters of my own fishbowl, who are outside the system of oppression that keeps me enslaved. I may rage against people, but that will change little. Or I may turn that rage against a system that upholds such prejudice and inequality. I may stand side-by-side with those most affected, not to try and save them but to learn from them.

This is key – that just as I recognise the influence of the system upon my life, I also recognise the deeper motivations that arise as my desire to change the world meets my need to try and save people. My motivations will always flow out of both the good within me and the shadow. I realised this most recently when a memory came flooding back to me.

~

If you have come here to help me, you are wasting our time. But if you have come because your liberation is bound up with mine, then let us work together.

Aboriginal Activists Group, Queensland, 1970s[18]

Damsel in distress

It was in a marketplace in Papua New Guinea where I first saw a woman smashed hard across the face. Assaulted. I was 15. She was older. A Papuan lady. I had sat down, an inquisitive teenager who loved talking with people and hearing their stories. But not today.

Her partner walked over and, ignoring me in mid-sentence, grabbed her ear and smashed her face with his fist. I still remember the blood. I still remember her being dragged away by the other women in the market. I still remember staring at the man who was double my size – me, a lanky, red-headed, freckly white boy who could do nothing. I froze. The man laughed. He turned and walked away. I shook for days.

What I remember most: the utter helplessness.

It was in a hotel in Papua New Guinea, the same trip, still 15. There was a girl, a pretty girl, the same age. Every night we talked, looking out at the world and the ocean, and part of me wanted to kiss her. I remember moonlight white on brown skin. Her face always slightly hidden.

On the final night I saw her, I sat listening to a CD on my Discman. She was crying, standing out by the water, looking out to sea. Next to her was a man fishing. I watched for a while until he left, then went to her. Slowly. She would not look up at me. Tears streaked her face. I hoped it was because I was leaving the next day, but it was not. The tears were because *she* had to stay. The tears were because every night she would go from our innocent conversations back to the reason she was at the hotel. The fisherman. A Frenchman. The hotel chef. She was his play thing. An object for him to rape every night. She could not leave, she told me. I wanted to tell someone, but she would not let me. It was her only way to survive.

Her story spilled out with the tears. They stained my skin. I tried to rub them away. They would not leave.

My brain also tried to rub her away. And literally, I did not remember this experience. It was blocked from my conscious memory – until a few months ago. Twenty years later, I was walking on the sand by the sea with a warm breeze and a familiar smell and a song that played through my headphones. It was a song I had played her that night, a CD in a Discman back then, Spotify now.

I let her listen hoping it would help, as the song had helped me. The fractured attempt of a teenage kid to do something in the midst of such atrocity.

Now, 20 years later, and the song and the ocean and the smell, and it all opened, and through the shadowed doorway of memory I could see her. The pretty girl. She came tumbling through the years, and I fell on my knees weeping for her. I could see it all. I could feel it all. I remembered the rage, how I wanted to kill that man. And I remembered crying myself to sleep that night.

But what I remember most: the utter helplessness.

~

Just a boy. Just a lanky, red-headed, freckly, white Australian boy who could do nothing. I froze, helpless. It is a feeling I have run from ever since.

And so I became a rescuer. A knight in shining armour.

A white knight in shining armour.

A white, male knight in shining armour bright for that poor damsel in distress.

But really, I just didn't want to feel helpless again. Incapable again. Powerless again.

To this day, I am still making up for the boy who liked a girl he had just met and had to leave her as a sex slave. I help the powerless so I do not have to feel powerless again. I need to name this in myself – this saviour complex. In all I do to help the world, I am just trying to help myself. To not have to feel so small. To stand tall.

We 'white, male knights in shining armour bright' all seem to talk too loudly. Walk too proudly. Set our posture too large. We take up too much space. We demand that the world build a shrine to its great white saviours. Look at us helping all these poor wretched souls, these damsels in distress! Look at how we bought these savages into civility!

Look at me, I am a super-hero-justice-warrior.

But really, we name *them* as helpless so that *we* don't have to feel so helpless. This is my prejudice. This is me. The water of the fishbowl I swim in still. I cannot escape from it. I am too big for my boots.

It is time to take off the shoes. It is time to take a knee. It is time to stop trying to rescue the world when I am really just trying to rescue me.

It is time to sit in the dust with those who sit in the dust and just listen. To learn. To hear their voice. To trust in the dignity of strong women, and of a strong people who have weathered more storms than I have even smelled. Let them teach these ignorant eyes what determination really means.

Please hear me. I will not stop doing what I can. This is not a call to apathy. But I have hurt too many people trying not to feel helpless, and I don't know if I can rid myself of such false motivation. It is a thorn in the flesh that will plague me all my days. The stains of her tears cannot be wiped away.

But may I choose today to lessen the grip such motivation has on me.

Starting with remembering her. Starting with forgiving myself. Starting with lowering myself to the ground and not believing I have all the answers and all the solutions for all the world's problems. Starting with allowing myself to feel incapable again.

I cannot save the world. There, I said it.

I am unable to bring about the change I desire to see.

You cannot save the world. Can you say it?

All you helpers. All you competent. All you rescuers. All you achievers.

You cannot save the world. And it is not your place to do so.

It is a white colonialist arrogance that believes we have the answers to what the Indigenous community in Australia, or the black community in the United States, or the masses fleeing persecution in Syria truly need.

These days I am trying to stop being a voice for the voiceless. I've come to see that too often the voiceless are ignored as they are spoken for, as we stand in front of them proudly claiming that we are 'saving the world' while stroking our own egos.

So I take a step back. I take a step down. I seek only to stand alongside, never in front of. I seek not to speak for but to do what I can to amplify the voice they themselves have. I need to hear it as much as anyone else.

They are not voiceless. We just need to listen.

We need to listen especially to those we do not understand. Those whose voice is muffled by the waters of the fishbowl we swim in.

Let us block out the white-noise, rich-noise, male-noise and do what we can to amplify her voice rather than our own. Every person has something to teach us. Every voice.

Let us name our own prejudice.

Let us speak only for ourselves and our reality, and create space for others to tell their story.

Let us embrace all we lack and find a grace within it.

The Fishbowl of Faith

And, remember, you were born into this. You asked Jesus into your heart, and you belonged to the Church People who had known you forever, who loved you like their own ... From there, Jesus became your thing, your own kind of extracurricular activity. You'd found your safe place, and you stayed there, burrowing deeper and deeper into it. You had God. You had Jesus the way other kids had soccer or drama or choir. You had youth group pizza parties and bike trips and weekend retreats ... It felt so big to you, that fire in your heart. It filled your body, gave you buoyancy and belonging. A send of purpose ... At fourteen, we believed in these things. Bigness. Numbers. Revival. We wanted a hundred people, a thousand people, a million different voices all saying the same thing ... We wanted everything.

Addie Zierman[19]

My church

The church of my younger years was a fishbowl. I didn't realise it at the time. But let me share here the waters that shaped me regardless.

Before I begin, I must admit this telling will be tainted by my movement out of this fishbowl, my unravelling from it, as much as by my time inside it. There will be those who also grew up in my church tradition whose experience will be far different from mine. There will be those who disagree with what I have written and say I have taken my critique too far. There will also be those who say I have not taken it far enough. Either way, for this bias I apologise. I cannot reflect apart from my own prejudiced experience, so I acknowledge it here. I acknowledge that some of these reflections still stem from the unraveled within me and therefore may come across as angry or cynical to some. Again, for this I apologise. Does this make them illegitimate thoughts? I don't think so. Does this make them biased? Absolutely. But I name this reality and ask you to not turn the reflections away and reject them because they are not how you have experienced things. May you learn from them how the unraveled can feel about their experience within the church.

My church was Anglican, contemporary, seeker-sensitive, white, middle-class, Bible-believing, Calvinist, mega-church-wanna-be (I told you I would be biased), evangelistic and evangelical. Don't worry if you are not from my tradition and do not know the meaning of these words. There will be more of them in this section. Just bear with me. Every fishbowl has a dictionary of insider terms. These were ours. It is hard to describe without using such words.

My church was home. A large home. This is what it felt like as a child. It was in this church that I cut my spiritual teeth. I knew every nook of that place. Hours of hide-and-seek and squashed sardines. It was where I first kissed a girl, in the loft of the church, behind the stage. My youth leaders never found out.

It was a church of brick and wood and lots of brown. Not the people, the paint. Lots of brown paint, lots of white people. I spent hours lying on pews counting the numbers of bricks leading up to the ceiling. My dad singing loud beside me. My mum talking with seemingly every person in the room.

The saints gathered in that place. They loved in that place. And how they loved. My church was a family. As a child I did not know the politics that also hung out behind the stage. All I knew from these many adults was a bestowal of acceptance and an inquiring into my life by the friends of my parents. I knew that I belonged there. I knew I was accepted.

I knew the grace of God in that church. It was taught often from the pulpit. And I also knew the fear of hell. I remember a sermon that as a child filled my imagination with fire and anguish and desperate people crying out for a drop of water where there was none to be found. I remember the nightmares that followed. I remember asking Jesus to save me from this hell. My childhood salvation – a mixture of love and grace and fear.

This was my church. Love. Grace. Fear. I grew up surrounded by it. Yet I was known and loved in that place. It was home.

I knew how to get lollies in Sunday school from the old ladies. I knew how to colour in Noah's ark as best I could. I knew the books of the Bible by memory. I knew the Apostles' Creed by memory. I knew Bible verses by memory. And I knew that all this memorising meant lollies. Striving to be the best each week also meant affirmation. To know the answers; to be the quickest to find the Bible passage; to be praised for it. A childhood spiritual pride. This was my childhood Christianity.

By the time I was a teenager, the childish pursuit of being commended by adults turned into the teenage pursuit of being affirmed by youth group leaders. To be seen as being on fire for God. A sold-out follower of Jesus. And I was good at it. I was seen as the spiritual one, the mature one, the one with his hands up in worship at the front of the church, the one who would become a youth pastor. My ego affirmed again and again.

In no way did I realise this was what was happening. I didn't realise much of it was my own performance. I didn't realise I was looking for the applause. I was a fish in a bowl and couldn't know my wetness. I felt the passion of being *on fire*. It was real. So I could not have named the shadow side of what came with this reality. I would have denied it if someone had pointed it out.

Yet hindsight is a great revealer. It is easy now to see how much performance and the desire for affirmation dictated my spiritual actions back then. The stoking of my teenage passion was interlinked with the stoking of my teenage ego. It is easy to see now how my church fishbowl was set up to create this performance-driven spirituality – this pressure to prove myself worthy, to live up to the cultural norms, to always try to be something.

And it is easy to see how much I still carry this mentality around within me, in my spirituality, my relationships, my vocation. I must achieve. I must succeed. It is a thorn in my flesh I constantly try to remove. Still it persists.

~

My church was orthodox. I grew up believing there was one set of answers and we were the ones who held them. Anyone who believed differently from us, well, they just had it wrong.

Mine was a fishbowl that prided itself on its adherence to 'biblical Christianity'. This was a mostly black-and-white Christianity. Right doctrine and proper teaching of the Bible were espoused as of utmost importance. Feelings and experiences in regards to faith were dubious at best, and outright deceptive at worst. What mattered was a reasoned understanding of the Bible, not some wishy-washy experiential hoo-ha.

Because of this, within my tradition, the Pentecostals and the charismatics were viewed with much suspicion. I remember the time a group of us young people were beginning to delve into a more charismatic posture towards our faith. I was asked into a meeting with the senior minister and the assistant minister, who gave me a thorough questioning about what was happening and shared how worried they were about it all.

The charismatics were not the only ones seen with suspicion. Social justice could too easily lead to a 'social gospel', a forgetting all about sin and the need for God's grace, so any justice-focused churches were also discounted.

The worst thing you could be in the world, worse even than an atheist, was a 'liberal' Christian. Liberal. It was a word always spoken with distaste, as in 'I heard those liberals don't even believe that Jesus rose from the dead.' I knew 'being a liberal' was bad well before I knew what 'being a liberal' meant. Or at least what it meant in the fishbowl of my church tradition. I was told what I needed to believe, and so I believed it in fear I would turn into one of those liberals.

This meant the Uniting Church in Australia was out, for they smelled like they could be 'liberal'. Probably they also only had a 'social gospel'. And some of their churches even had gay people in them. That was definitely a no-no in my tradition.

Baptists were OK. We just didn't know why they had to insist on full-immersion baptism.

And Catholics, well, we weren't even sure they could be called Christians. In fact, I was told by my minister they were not Christians, all because they upheld different beliefs to my fishbowl's.

No, the only true Bible-believing tradition was our own.

Sadly, I am not joking. Sometimes explicitly and always implicitly, this was what was taught to us.

In fact, these were the exact words the archbishop at the time used to try to convince me that I should only study at the college of my denomination. When he heard I was thinking about going to a different theological seminary, he sat me down, told me why all the other denominational colleges were inept in their exegesis of Scripture and advised that if I didn't want to be fooled, I should study with his college. He told me blatantly it was the only true Bible-believing college in Australia.

I did not go to his college.

~

My church was comfortable. Literally. It was designed that way. Seeker-sensitive. The whole approach was to make the church service as user-friendly as possible and the youth group as cool as possible, and thereby to convert people. Attract the masses. Numbers matter.

The Bible studies were meant to be where the deeper things were discussed, but unless you had a particularly well-thought-out, engaged and well-read leader, most of the time these were spent talking about the answers we already knew. An echo chamber. There were times, though, when you would come across a leader who broke the mould. A young adult who was willing to push things further. A contingent of adults within the church who would open your eyes to a new way of seeing something. How refreshing that was! Indeed, perhaps these people were some of the first who helped me to start asking questions. I remember when my youth pastor went through his own time of questioning, his own unravelling. I learned more from him during this season than I had ever learned before.

But the main model was seeker-sensitive. We wanted to save as many people as possible. And those with the power, those in charge of the church, needed to keep the church running. It was a neat and ordered system based on people coming to church and giving money to the church and using their gifts in the church to keep the wheels of the church well oiled. A machine.

I cannot remember hearing talks that directly challenged consumerism and the Western Dream, that critiqued middle-class lifestyles, that talked of caring for the earth, that spoke of giving your life on behalf of the outcast and the marginalised. The message of 'sell everything you have and follow me' (Matthew 19:21) was too uncomfortable. So it was always somehow watered down to giving your time and energy to the church, and 10 percent of your income to keep the church running.

It was a Christianity solely focused on individual salvation, on growing in one's vertical relationship with a spiritual God, and on then being a good moral person and trying to convert people. It was a Christianity that ignored the radical social and economic calling of Jesus. The social was made spiritual. Jesus was turned into a spiritual saviour who came to die for one's sins, rather than the subversive social dissident killed as a political insurrectionist, as one claiming to be King, as one opposed to the Caesar, as one standing against the oppressive systems of the day.

So I was never taught about standing against the oppressive systems of our day. I was never taught how my Christianity must affect my relationship with the Indigenous people of the land, with the refugee, with the corporations of Western culture, with the slaves who make our clothes in factories overseas. I was not taught about social systems at all.

It is Tom Sine who says that most Western Christianity is just 'the American dream with a thin overlay of Jesus'.[20] I sadly agree. So many who are zealous in pushing their beliefs as absolute (be they about the Bible, morals, sexuality or religion) do not see anything wrong with their wealthy lifestyle in the face of following a Jesus who spent his life on behalf of the marginalised of his society and explicitly told us to do the same.

~

My church was patriarchal. Men were taught that they were the leaders of their household, that they had the final say. 'Headship' it was called, and is still called today. The justifying rhetoric was that women are equal to men in personhood but have different functions, functions that do not include teaching and leading men.

So the leaders and the pastors of my church were all male. This was not by accident. Women were not allowed to be ordained. They were not allowed to become preachers. This was a direct result of a particularly literal reading of certain Scripture verses and an ignoring of others.[21] Or rather, it was an upholding of the verses that affirmed the cultural position already held. Out of cultural and textual context, you can use single verses from the Christian Scriptures to uphold almost any ideology you wish. Every Christian fishbowl does this; it is inevitable.

So while *I* could become a minister and lead the people and preach to the masses, the best my female friends wanting to 'go into ministry' could hope for was to be a children's minister or an administrator, or perhaps to run the music teams (no disrespect to any of these). They would not lead the men. They were not given the power to do so.

Yet I knew women who certainly would have been much better preachers than the men in my church. And I knew women who would have been far better pastors and leaders than the men in my church. They did not get the chance. All because they 'had a different function.' It was (and is) a great loss to the church. It was a great loss to my life growing up.

I was also told that when I grew up, I would take the headship of my family. I would be able to make decisions for my household, and though I should certainly listen to my wife's perspective, it would be up to me in the end. I would be the one with the power. And yet, again, I could see all around me strong women who could (and in reality did) lead households much better than their husbands ever could. I now realise this meant that while the wives had all the responsibility and actually managed the household, the men still held all the power.

~

My church was concerned, and rightly so. Concerned about the effect our society was having on its young people. Not consumer culture; we were not taught about that. It was mostly concerned about our sexual purity.

Sex was something that belonged solely in marriage. Sexuality was about 'what you did with your bits.' So what we heard from the men on the stage was to do whatever we could to not have sex, and in the

45

meantime to not give in to sexual temptation in any way. The girls were cautioned again and again not to wear revealing clothing, not to make the boys stumble. Their body, they were told implicitly, was something that would bring sin into the world.

The boys were told not to look lustfully at the girls and the girls were told not to make the boys lust after them. Sexual drive was seen as something only suitable after matrimony, so any hint of it beforehand, any sexual thought or desire, had to be blocked out. Recite a Bible verse, shield your mind, whatever it took to stay completely pure.

However, since the teenage brain is innately wired to receive a huge increase in sex hormones during and after puberty, an increase that naturally and inevitably leads to sexual desires and sexual fantasies, this meant that such an approach only led many of us boys into dark spirals of shame. We fought hard against the biologically natural process of our bodies. We attempted the impossible. Both sexes came to believe that any hint of sexual arousal within them was something to be exterminated. The boys talked about it at least, but I am not sure the girls even had the space to.

The pendulum swung from the world of pornography and advertising, which takes sexuality and cheapens it into smut, to seeing sexuality as something wrong, something perverted (unless you were married). Instead of being taught a healthy understanding and embracing of our sexuality before marriage, instead of being taught that sexuality is so much more than 'what you do with your bits', for us sexuality became something to be hidden and starved. A separation of spirituality from physicality. A fear of the sensual. Shame. Guilt. Hiddenness.

There were many closets and skeletons – especially for those whose sexuality didn't fit. I remember once in later life going back to the church and the couple who told me in whispers about their son who had just come out of the closet. They told me they really wanted to support him, they wanted to stand alongside him whatever his sexual orientation, but they knew what this meant. It meant going against the teachings of the church. So they stepped into the closet their son has just stepped out of. They kept it all hidden for fear of what others would think. Closets and skeletons.

When there is only one way to be and any other way is wrong; when there is no safe space for discussion and disagreement and challenge; when we do not listen well to those outside our fishbowl – then there will always be closets and skeletons. They hide those too afraid to show their difference.

~

My church was evangelistic. We young people wanted to see our generation saved. We wanted to see the world come to know Jesus. We had a youthful enthusiasm coupled with a dose of teenage arrogance, a litre of white colonialism and a whole swag of zeal.

We were taught a gospel presentation to convert people. It had 100 points to it including verses and illustrations and questions to ask, and we memorised the whole thing. We would go out on weekends trying to get into conversations where we could share this entire 100-point memorised presentation.

I passionately tried to convert my friends at school, and how proud I was when two rows of pews in my church were filled with these friends. My youth leaders noticed. My youth minister noticed. My minister noticed. I didn't realise how much their 'notice' drove the motivation. It was one more form of spiritual performance.

But it felt good. I wasn't just a sheep inside the fence. This sheep was on fire. I was burning bright and beautiful.

I went on mission trips to share the 100-point gospel presentation with the world. Vanuatu. Papua New Guinea. Fiji. Samoa. Tonga. Indonesia. Every year I would go with the other young Christians of my church, and we would gather in planes and buses singing our church songs as we went, feeling so full of purpose and so in line with God. We would be the ones to see revival come. When the trips ended, we would report back to the church on the number of converts, and we would feel the holy pride, and be unable to understand why others didn't get how important this work was. Couldn't they see we were making a difference?

We were making a difference.

I am sure we were.

In both good ways and bad ways, we were making a difference.

We went to train pastors and church leaders in how they could use this gospel presentation. Our mindset was 'they don't need white missionaries to come over and do this; they can do it themselves if they're taught how.' But a 15-year-old white boy from a completely different culture teaching a grown man how to share his faith in his own culture, a culture that I literally knew nothing about …? I didn't realise it at the time, but something was decidedly off with this picture.

One of the main problems with my posture on these trips was that I never really noticed the people I was talking to. I did not really see them and the actuality of their lives. I did not listen to them. Instead I spoke *at* them. I dumped a pre-packaged, 100-point memorised gospel presentation at their feet and told them to pray a prayer to accept Jesus into their lives. I did not go to learn from them what following Jesus looked like. I never let the reality of their lives challenge the reality of my own. And I certainly never wondered what might actually be the good news for them.

The colonialist, evangelical 15-year-old missionary. That was me.

African American author and speaker Lisa Sharon Harper has stated, 'For the good news to be good news, then it has to actually be good news … a good news for all peoples, the starving, the broken, the oppressor and the oppressed.'[22] That is, for a good news to be good news to an oppressed people, it must speak also to a history of slavery and prejudice. It cannot ignore the reality of their lives and history. So when we turn to the actuality of the world and its oppressed peoples, what does the good news sound like? What does it sound like to the enslaved African, to the mother whose child has just been taken, to the women raped, to the Indigenous of the land? What does it sound like to all the colonised peoples of this world? What does the good news have to say to them?

And please, please, before you answer this question, I beg of you: do not. Do not answer it. This will be your first inclination. Resist it. Instead go and ask. Go and listen. Take a step away from your fishbowl.

~

My church was fenced. One of the ways that any community defines who it is, is by defining who it is not. I knew who I was as a good evangelical and I certainly knew who I wasn't. Other denominations were viewed with suspicion and other religions were simply pitied, for they had been duped.

I belonged inside the fence as a child because I was born into it. I belonged inside the fence in my teens because I believed the right things and I behaved the right way. This was the litmus test. If you upheld the correct doctrine and the cultural code of conduct then you were 'one of us'.

It was just like sheep. Sheep inside a fence.

Michael Frost and Alan Hirsch write that the shape of spiritual community can be seen in how farmers hold sheep.[23] When you keep sheep on a farm, you can either fence them in so they have no way to escape or, if you have a large enough property, place a drinking well at the centre of the property that the sheep won't wander far from. When you use a drinking well, you have no need for the fences.

Sheep farming is analogous to a community of faith. Some uphold a fenced version of faith, demanding that people stay within the fences of correct doctrine and correct behaviour – the fences of what one *should* look like if they are to be a part of such a community. You know who you are by the fences that surround you.

As a young evangelical I knew the fences clearly, both the explicit ones and the implicit ones. The fences of behaviour and the fences of belief.

The fences of behaviour: go to church, youth group and Bible study once a week. Don't smoke. Don't drink. Don't have sex before marriage. Don't lust. Don't be a practising homosexual. Listen to Christian music. Try to convert your friends.

The fences of doctrine: beautiful doctrines around grace and the utter, unequivocal love of God; doctrines about a relational trinitarian Godhead; doctrines about each and every person made in the image of God.

There were doctrines too that I have certainly wrestled with and changed my thinking upon since that time. Doctrines like 'original sin'

– that all of us are born sinful; 'substitutionary atonement' – that Jesus paid the penalty we sinners deserved by taking on himself the wrath of God (a doctrine taught to us as the only correct way of interpreting the work of Jesus on the cross); 'predestination' – that God chose people, predestined them, for heaven and therefore also predestined others to hell. And of course, there was the doctrine of a literal hell for eternity for anyone who did not believe what we did.

These and many, many more were the things we simply believed and did. We did not question. Why would we? This was the truth. For most of my teens I had no idea you could believe anything different and still call yourself a Christian.

If you believed the right things and behaved the right way, then you *belonged*. We knew what we needed to do, and we knew what happened if we didn't do it. We knew the stories of the fallen, the hushed stories told over campfires about friends who started dating non-Christians and ended up on drugs. Evangelical ghost stories. Within the peer-group setting of high school, if you don't believe or look or act the same as your clique, you are simply cast out and seen as uncool. Within the Christian faith, however, those who do not adhere to the prescribed doctrine and behaviour are given labels. Backslidden. Liberal. Fallen away. These labels are a carried-over threat from family life: 'If you live under my roof you will …'

The Sculpted Self, then, is very concerned with who is in and who is out. It wants to draw the boundaries of right and wrong and enforce such delineation. If you agree with me you may remain; if not, then you are on the outer. The Sculpted Self fights to prove the authority of its fishbowl. The fishbowl then becomes a fortress.

The threat of exclusion – be it in an adolescent peer group, an adult workplace or a religious community – breeds a fervent and diehard following. An us-versus-them mentality. Those in the community thoroughly embrace the social rules and hide those things that don't match up. They give up their own distinctiveness. They ignore any thoughts that may be contrary to the community of which they are a part. They put on the mask of pretence.

My church was masked. Many there couldn't live up to the standard. Many felt they had to hide. Many squashed down their true thoughts and feelings and questions and doubts. Many wore their Sunday-best smiles while their lives were falling apart. So many closets. So many skeletons.

WWJD

This is who we were back then. This is who *I* was back then. Admittedly, it was a mixture of my church and the pervasive presence of the American evangelical system of the '90s packaged through the magazines I read and the music I listened to. It all came together to form my cultural Christianity.

But what a Christianity it was. We were passionate. We were filled with purpose. We were going to do amazing things for God. This we knew for certain. Our insider culture made us feel different from the rest of the world, special, chosen. We had God on our side. We were right and they were wrong.

Even their music was wrong. I got rid of my secular albums during my passionate teenage years. Metallica and Pantera albums burnt down by the creek near our house. Instead, as in any fishbowl defined by social artefacts, we listened to our own music. Jars of Clay. Audio Adrenaline. *I* knew all the words to DC Talk's 'Jesus Freak' (still do), and I would dance around to it in my room yelling the words out to the walls, my face covered in passionate tears: 'I don't really care if they label me a Jesus Freak/There ain't no disguising the truth/No, I ain't hiding the truth.' This was me declaring my allegiance to this Jesus, declaring how I would follow him with my whole life even if my school friends didn't understand. I would do it. And I did it.

But here was the problem. I didn't realise that what I was declaring my allegiance to looked more like the evangelical fishbowl of the '90s than a rebellious Jewish man named Jesus.

During my teenage years a marketing fad took off in the evangelical world: WWJD wrist bands. WWJD stood for 'What Would Jesus Do?' The bands were meant as a reminder, in any situation, to ask yourself this question and then to act accordingly. A nice attempt at a quasi-ethical framework for teenage Christians, aimed at moving them on from choosing actions solely based on self-interest.

Yet, as a Western teenager asking this question, I was not in reality seeking to imitate exactly what this Jewish man of 2000 years ago did. A simplistic repetition of Jesus' life would have meant an adherence to the Jewish traditions of that time. It would have meant not getting married or having children. It would have meant so many things I was not prepared to actually do – that no Christ-follower is prepared to actually do. So rather than imitating Jesus, it was instead an uneducated speculation about what Jesus might do in my current situation.

The problem was that the Jesus I was asking the question of looked a whole lot like me.

I am a white man. And this white skin is an emblem of my privilege. I did not know this back then – could not have known it, like the fish could not know its wetness.

If those around us serve as a mirror as to who we should be in this world, around me all I could see was white. My childhood was white. My high school was white. My church was white. My pastors were white. Later in life my theology college was white. My professors were white. My theology books were white. So inevitably, throughout my life my theology has been white. My Bible has been white. My Jesus has been white. My God has been white.

I have painted the world with this one colour for too long.

We have painted the world with this one colour for too long.

My Jesus was white and my Jesus was middle class and my Jesus was Western, and so my Jesus was domesticated. My Jesus was concerned about the spiritual and moral things of life (which for a teenage boy were mainly about not lusting over girls), but not about the gross social and economic inequalities of the world and how I might perpetuate these.

This is the Jesus you end up with when you read Jesus solely from the perspective of the privileged. Those in the mansion on the hill. Privilege dictates a certain understanding of the world and of the sacred texts and of the Divine. I cannot help but read the Christian Scriptures (or any other text) through the lens of being a middle-class, white, heterosexual man swimming around in his fishbowl. In my teenage years, I didn't realise that while I may have one answer as to what Jesus might do with any particular contemporary issue, someone else swimming in a slightly different fishbowl may have a completely different answer. The conservative, right-wing evangelical will deduce a different answer from the progressive, left-wing Catholic, or the Guatemalan mother, or the Iraqi father.

So not surprisingly, when I asked 'WWJD?' I ended up with answers that validated all of my biases.

The reality for those of us who are Christian is that we spend much time simply trying to get Jesus to say what we want him to say. To get him to support the status-quo safety of our fishbowl.

As has been said in the past, 'God made us in his image and then we went and returned the favour.'

If you grew up 200 years ago as a white Anglo-Saxon in Western society, it is highly likely you would have believed that dark-skinned people were a lower form of human, and therefore that it was perfectly fine to own them as slaves. You would have believed this because it was what the majority of white fishbowls believed at the time – often validating it, sadly, by their interpretation of the Christian Scriptures.

These ideas in the wider fishbowl of Western society have now changed. There are few who would actively condone slavery. And yet, just like the Christians who are Christian because they have grown up Christian, or the atheists who are atheist because their parents were atheist, we too have grown up being taught this societal ethic about slavery and equality. It is the implicitly agreed upon norm. And yet, if the society around us still believed differently as it did 200 years ago, most of us would also believe differently.

We know this because although the vast majority of us would adamantly state we believe slavery is wrong, the reality is that all of us condone slavery by our actions. We wear clothing made by slaves.

We use computers made by slaves. We eat food farmed by slaves. The rhetoric of what we say we believe is far different from the reality of our lifestyles. We say we oppose slavery, yet the affluence of our society can only exist because someone down the line is not treated equally. We indirectly perpetuate slavery with our actions.

This is a form of what George Orwell calls 'doublethink'. 'Doublethink' is where we trick ourselves into ignoring the great chasm between our rhetoric and our reality. It is too uncomfortable to admit the incongruences. That we are prejudiced towards those who are different. That we see them as less. That we place ourselves before the other.

We *need* to be taught that slavery is wrong. We *need* to be taught all we are taught by our sculpting communities. I needed my church. I needed my family table. Whether you heard glimpses of your own story as I described mine or whether yours was wildly different, either way, you too were in a fishbowl. Either way, it sculpted the way you see the world. This was the only way for both of us to begin. The fishbowl and the table are inescapable.

The problem is that the fishbowl and the table can only get us so far.

There is the theology I want to believe, that I think I believe … and then there is the theology I actually practice.

Kenda Creasy Dean[24]

The Fishbowl of Truth

What labels me, negates me.

Søren Kierkegaard[25]

Idols and absolutes

To live out of the Sculpted Self is to know the things you know beyond a shadow of a doubt, but to not have thought through where such absolute knowledge comes from.

During my sculpted upbringing, I could quote a plethora of Bible verses at people when they posed questions to me. An exhaustive list of the right answers. I saw questions as something to be definitively answered so as to convince the person of the rightness of my beliefs. Questions were not opportunities for my own growth or a springboard into new ways of thinking and being. They were opportunities to enforce my particular belief system. The Sculpted Self is the thesis, the answer, the conclusion.

In hindsight, sitting beneath much of this desire to be right was simply the desire to be in control. To stay safe. When the world is full of unanswerable questions, it can be a scary place. Faith is the same. So instead we run to the definitive answer to be our fortress. The Sculpted Self then becomes obsessed with what is truth and what is not. It may be an implicit obsession, but it is still present. The Sculpted Self does not reach further than its own boundaries; it cannot see further than the glass of the fishbowl. It becomes short-sighted, defensive and guarded.

If you are from the Christian faith, as I am, you likely hold that your particular beliefs come straight from the Bible and are therefore absolute. In reality, your beliefs come from the particular biblical interpretation given by your specific Christian tradition, mixed in with the influence of your culture. You believe what you do because you have been shaped to believe it. You read the Bible through a particular lens. Other people who are just as devoted, just as exegetically astute, just as 'biblical', but who are from a different tradition of thought, will read the very same Scripture and come to a different conclusion.

We bring our fishbowl-tinted, coloured lenses to every text we read or engage with, be it a Shakespearean sonnet, a contemporary movie, a scientific book that proves evolution, a religious book, or simply the text of our everyday lives. How we interpret the words of our lover or the words of a sacred text comes through the same channels of interpretation. We bring our bias to the table and cannot help but read our context into the text, just as the author's context was written into the text. That is a lot of filters that a text passes through before it is comprehended by the reader. A lot of fuzziness in any communication.

The Sculpted Self finds this a very difficult proposition – that our claims to Truth are in fact inevitably shaped by our culture. It is a humbling thing to admit our own finiteness in the wake of our own bias.

I wonder, then, if truth is *not* something we should be using as a weapon to push our own worldview. I wonder if truth should never be used as proof of one's own rightness. I wonder if truth is actually something far greater than just being 'right'.

Those firmly in a sculpted understanding of the world tend to bluff-off how Disney and MTV have shaped their theology. How particular ways of thinking have shaped their faith without them even realising. How their parents' and peers' understandings of the world have directly influenced their own. How their culture has enforced over and over a worldview that is most comfortable to them.

The danger then lies in our addiction to the comfort that this brings, to the soft padding and simplistic world of unexamined belief. Fixed and certain, ordered and secure, bounded within a frame. Our claims to absolute Truth leave us ignorant as to what we may find on the other side of the fishbowl glass – what is out there where the world doesn't make as much sense.

If we defend our fishbowls as absolute, they become the very thing that inhibits our further movement. They become our safety and our crutch. When we think we are so sure of our answers, we are in fact hindered from realising the real point of it all. As a student of mine once said in class, 'I am in bondage to the things I think I know.'

Our absolutes become our idols.

When I speak of God, I am not speaking of God but of my own conception of God. Not that this means there is no Truth about God; rather it means I can never fully grasp such absolute Truth because I cannot get away from my own bias in favour of my particular understanding of God. Yet if I claim this understanding as absolute, I make it into an idol.

When we do not name, explore and examine our beliefs, then our perspective holds us captive. If we claim our understanding is fixed and we have the answers, we stop asking the questions, we stop listening, we stop searching, we stop wrestling, we stop growing. We let the dust settle around our certainty and our ego. We succumb to the security of non-movement, the safety of being stuck.

Black and white is safe. It is just not reality.

When our inherited and socialised beliefs are never consciously examined, we stand at the edge of a slippery slope. If I am someone who buys into the values of the people and society around me, I lose myself in the shape of everybody else. A chameleon coloured by its external environment. When those around me change, so do I. A teenager who grows up going to church on Sundays, youth group on Fridays, Bible study on a weeknight and Christian schooling every day of the week is socialised into Christianity, and if they do not question why they hold their beliefs, when the socialising forces change, they will chameleon into whatever the next thing is.

The label and the box

For some of you reading my background above, the words 'conservative evangelical Christianity' may feel like home. They may bring comfort and a sense of security. For you, the easy step from here would be to do what we do best: place this writer in a box of 'too progressive' or 'too liberal' and then take a hammer to the box.

For others these words may instead induce a metallic distaste in the back of your throat, a pit in your stomach, a gag reflex of resistance. For you, the easy step from here would be to do what we do best: place this writer in a box of everything you think about conservative evangelical Christianity and then take a hammer to the box.

I have been placed in many such boxes. I place others in such boxes. They are hard to escape from. We love our systems and our labels and our cardboard walls. They allow us to not have to deal with the complexities of real-life, flesh-and-blood people. We simply ignore them and bring a critique to the construct that we have placed them inside.

However, I am Joel McKerrow. I am a husband. I am a writer. I am a friend. I am a teacher. I was born into conservative evangelical Christianity and it has decidedly shaped me whether you like it or not, whether I like it or not. It has shaped me both in terms of what I have taken on board from it and what I have rebelled against in it. I am both its pattern and the inverse of its pattern. This is who wrote this book. A real person. A true person.

I am Joel McKerrow. I doubt myself often, but I push past these doubts. I feel guilty that I am not doing a good enough job in the roles I live out. I do not have life together, that's for certain. I look for affirmation from others to stroke my ego. I dream of bringing change to this world and feel often that I fall short. I am made of this shadow and I am made of this light. This is who wrote this book. Not a label that you would like to place on me.

We do this all the time in my country. On those seeking asylum from war-torn nations we place a label like 'illegal immigrant' or 'queue jumper'. This label then allows us to forget about the life of a mother who, like any of us, is doing everything she can to try and keep her family alive. Instead we make up policies about the nebulous construct 'illegal immigrants'.

We also do this with those passionate about the equal rights of women: 'those raving feminists'; those passionate about the environment: 'those tree-hugging hippies'; those passionate about the equal rights of the foetus: 'those damn conservative pro-lifers'; those passionate about a woman's right to choose: 'those baby killers'; those passionate about faith: 'those brainwashed religious nuts.'

Labelling is our way of choosing not to listen to those who are not of our fishbowl. Those liberals. Those Democrats. Those Muslims. Those atheists. Those Christians. Those fundamentalists. Those progressives. I am as guilty as anyone of this. I label what makes me uncomfortable, what I do not understand. I absolutely acknowledge this book does the same.

Life, though, is not as simple as this labelling. Truth is not as simple as this. People are not as simple as this. I am not as simple as this. We strip a person of their humanity when we cast them in this light. We take away their real-life, complex and nuanced story in favour of our binaries. We stop listening to what may be our saving grace – the view from outside our fishbowl.

The sculpted within us holds a fear of what lies 'out there' and how it may spoil the pure water that is 'in here'. So we hold on, white knuckled. Bring up the walls. Defend our position. The Sculpted Self holds us tightly and we get wrapped up in tape. We fear what is different to us and so we box it. Label it. Masking tape and black ink.

We are so protective of our fishbowls. They are the ways we have constructed our world. So when someone shakes our bowl and tries to point out that we may in fact be something called 'wet', we tend to stop listening to them and start arguing with them. We turn that person into a label and rubbish the label. We place them in a box and tear apart the box.

The label and the box. We use them to make a complicated world easier to control. We fear a world that is not under our thumb.

To claim to hold the absolute truth of a thing is to place a label on that thing. When it comes to the unfathomable reality of God or Love or Grace – or really, anything spiritual – these labels are measly descriptors at best. They are words seeking to communicate the incomprehensible. All language, after all, is metaphor: sounds and markings that seek to describe a truth far greater than the sounds and markings could ever truly communicate.

My definition of *love*, even if it were the most articulate, well-thought-out expression about love ever penned, will still be just a small percentage of what love actually is.

It is the same with my definition of God. We say the names of God, we write them on his forehead, yet they are not the totality of who God is; they are not the Truth. The Truth is far greater. These names define our way of seeing the sacred more than they define the infinite God. Anything spoken, anything written, can only ever be seen as finite, as smaller than Truth. The Truth lies behind the label of our language in the undefinable place. The place where God exists. The place where reality holds its own.

Side-by-side (part 2)

Back now to chipped purple fingernails that sank slowly into tepid water. Glistening soap suds. Fingers that scrubbed away the food. They mingled there, her fingers, washed clean with the saucers and the cups.

'The years don't clean away so easily now, do they?'

We were standing side-by-side washing dishes at the kitchen sink of a drop-in centre for street workers. Side-by-side. As her comment floated out there in the space between us, I allowed myself to see the incongruence of my rhetoric and my reality. I allowed myself to feel it. Side-by-side, the good Christian boy and the street worker. Before this day, she didn't have a name. She was just a prostitute. She lived in a world that may as well have belonged on another planet. Side-by-side. My sheltered teenage existence and her fight-to-survive reality. Side-by-side.

I realised on this day that although I had grown up in a Christian family and had called myself a 'Christ-follower', although I had been such a passionate 'Jesus Freak', although I had spent so much time in Christian culture, this was actually the first time I had ever spent any real time with the people that Jesus spent all his time with. The highly marginalised in society. Those seen as lesser. Those struggling to make it in this harsh world.

That day, as I stared at her face rainbow-mirrored in the sink bubbles, I realised I was not a Christ-follower at all. I had simply been swimming in the waters of my Christian upbringing. I was a Christian because that was the faith I was brought up in. It was what I had inherited. What I had been socialised into.

My life, however, did not look like the life of Christ. I believed the right things, I had taken on all the appendages of '90s Christian evangelicalism, I upheld the doctrines of my fishbowl, and that was what was mirrored back to me. But now her face was mirrored next to mine. Each bubble in the sink reflected back to me a picture of both of us. I looked trapped in there. In the bubble. Frozen.

I caught a glimpse of myself swimming. The fishbowl of my family. The fishbowl of Western society. The fishbowl of my faith. The fishbowl of my truth. In that moment, washing dishes, I could see it. The smallness of the fishbowl I swam in.

The fishbowl cracked. A hairline down its side.

Just like digging a grave in Thailand, this experience was a contradiction with no easy solution. My bubble existence peeled back for me to see the world as it truly is. I saw that the names and labels I had given many things in my life, including this lady, were made up of a bias and a bigotry born of my ignorance.

I came face-to-face with my own incongruence. The things I did that I did not want to do. The things that came from beliefs I wished I did not have. The places where my gods resided whether I liked it or not. The theology I upheld whether I realised it or not. The reality of my life – comfortable, middle-class, Western, white. The reality of my Jesus – comfortable, middle-class, Western, white. The privileged paintbrush in my hand.

I came face-to-face with the hypocrisy in my own culture and faith, and I hated what I saw.

That day, without even realising it, I asked myself the question, 'If a fish in a bowl doesn't know that it is wet, then a Joel in the fishbowl of his family, his society, his faith, his truth, doesn't know … what?'

That day, I stared intently at two faces mirrored back in the bubble.

I stared and I stared. Button shirt next to too-short skirt.

And I realised I was trapped in a bubble, and in this realisation the bubble popped. The fishbowl smashed. My too-small world crumbled away. I felt an anger rise up inside me at all the hypocrisy in the world. It was all Hulk-like and ready to rage. My clothes stretched too tight. They split at the seams. The great unravelling had begun.

On Moving On

This is for the day when you are torn in two.
When the discontent comes.
When a world once endless
      is now four walls and closing.
The constriction of breath
and the whisper out ahead,
      there must be more than this.

This is for when the old ways can no longer hold you.
For when you realise
they have not been able to
      for quite some time now.

This is for the day of dissatisfaction.
The drip of a tap that is no longer flowing,
A nest too small.
      Throw yourself from her,
      flap wings even when you think that you have none.
I have seen men give themselves to this.
I have seen women.

She gave herself to flight, like falling was never an option.

This is for the day of choosing,
      itchy feet and shaking knees,
      clothes that stretch too small
      stringent borders and high prison walls.
The streets that knew us and gave us our name.
There is a silent death should you remain.

So walk out the door,
> leave the house of your conditioning,
> follow the path around the back,
>> through the fields.
> Though regret may follow you there,
> though fear and sorrow may be your guide for a time,
> keep walking.

They will soon lose interest
when they realise
that you have lost interest in them.

Take off your too tight skin.
The loss of our covering,
unravelling, raw and vulnerable and fraying at the edges.

This is for the day when change comes to find you.
When you smell a new scent on the wind.

This is for the day when they cannot hold you,
when you realise the rules were never made for you.

I urge you,
on that day
> to turn around, quickly now, not for too long
> take a picture with your mind,
> or this is the last time that you shall come back to
> this place.

Thank it for what it was,
the words given to you.
For who you became under its soft gaze,
pay it the homage it is due.
Tattoo its memory on the underside of your ribs,
       so that if the future takes everything from you,
       it can never take this
It may help you remember who you are in the face of such loss.

But for now turn from this,
give yourself to the new path,
the uncharted and the unfamiliar,
keep the wind at your back,
your pack is light and the night is over.

This is for the day when you take that first step
       and then the next.

Part 2:
The Unravelled Self

A Boat Story (continued)

The boy was given a boat. A wooden boat. A small boat for a small boy. The problem was that the harbour now felt small too. Everywhere he looked was the same as it had always been. He felt restless.

So every day he would creep closer and closer to the mouth of the harbour, feeling the pull of the open ocean. Everyday his father would call him back to the shore. Back to safety.

That is, until one day. A day like any other day. The boy got closer to the mouth of the harbour than he had been before. He looked over to see his father momentarily distracted. The boy turned his little boat to face the open ocean and sailed right out of that harbour.

A fire burned in his chest. The wind blew through his hair. Salt on his lips. There was a freedom he had never known. He was alive. It was wonderful.

He told himself he would go out just a little way more and then turn back in. But as the great unfamiliar surrounded him, he decided to go a bit further to see what he could see. A little further. The wind was pushing in the perfect direction. A little further.

A dolphin slid up beside his little boat and soared out of the water. He followed, mesmerised, until the dolphin dipped down out of view and disappeared.

The boy looked around. He could not see the harbour anymore. He could not even see land anymore. He could see nothing but blue ocean.

Panic gripped him. He pulled down the sail to stop being taken out any further. He turned the boat around and began to paddle straight back against the breeze. But by now it had really started to pick up. His paddling was getting him nowhere. Within minutes he was exhausted. Still he kept trying. Nothing. He wasn't even sure he was heading in the right direction.

The wind came wilder and wilder still. So did the ocean. The little boat was not built for this weather. Soon he was being tossed around by the waves. He would rush down one side and climb a green mountain of water on the other. Lobbed from one mountain to another. Giants on the peaks. Giants in the sea. The rain fell, the wind howled and the boy could only hold on for dear life.

A wave rose up before him, and this time he knew the little boat would not reach the top. He took a deep lungful of air, held his breath and the wave came at him.

Unravelled

Once upon a time you had it all beautifully sorted out. Then you didn't ... Bewildered. Baffled. Caught between what-was and what-will-be. Walking away from something perhaps, but not quite sure where you're even headed.

Sarah Bessey[26]

There really *must* be more than this

In the early days, when it all began to unravel, I took an early morning walk. I was in Sydney at the time and ended up down by a strip of shops at the beach in Manly. The day had just begun. A yawning morning. The sun was blinding. I was window gazing and looking for breakfast.

Instead, I met Joe.

Halfway down the strip I glanced to my left, and there, sitting hunched against a wall, was an old man. A rough beard sprouting from an unclean face. A mass of messy hair, matted with dirt and spent time. Tattered clothes. Bent back. Skin wrinkled and pulled tight around bones. A black beanie slumped down over his forehead. He was sitting next to a bow-legged walking frame, just holding its own under the weight of green and white shopping bags. I gathered he was homeless, his presence a stark contrast to the glitz of the stores and boutiques all around.

Joe was a lonely man. He had walked the pavement for years, the sort of dirty smudge most choose to ignore. And I had always been the type to ignore, conditioned not to see the ones in front of my face if they looked different to me. At any other moment in my life I would simply have kept walking. I may have felt sorry for him, possibly would have thrown a dollar in his cup if he had been begging. But certainly nothing more.

Yet things had begun to change in me.

The person I used to be felt like he didn't really exist anymore. Yet I had no idea who it was that did still exist. I was caught between two worlds, the past paradigms of faith that were unravelling all around me and a new beginning not yet strong enough to stand upon. I had no idea whether I still wanted to follow this Jesus I had always claimed to follow. I had no idea whether I even believed in God.

It was a liminal space. An in-between space. A threshold.

One world was falling away but the other had not yet been found. The fishbowl had shattered, yet sometimes I felt like I was still trapped in its small frame. And sometimes I felt like I was swimming lost in an ocean. Lost and Dory.[27] I couldn't remember who I was supposed to be.

My digging of the grave, my washing of dishes: these events were the first falling dominoes of a toppled existence. They were the beginning of the end of the old me. They were the lighting of a fuse that began an explosion, or perhaps an implosion, of the faith and lifestyle and worldview that had always been mine. Once sturdy foundations were now flimsy and shaken.

During the unravelling, I knew who I didn't want to be anymore. I just didn't know how to become someone new.

Hence it was an exasperated person who walked down the road in Manly that day. Discouraged and restless, disappointed and scared. With a burgeoning freedom and a feeling of loss. Doubtful, and yet somehow hopeful. Angry, and yet somehow excited. I was a confused mess of fear and passion, and as always, the shame that I wasn't doing life and faith right.

I just wish someone had told me that all of this was OK. That I was OK. That there was no need for the shame.

(Perhaps this is what you need today, too – someone like me, right now, to say to you: 'It will be OK, friend. You will be OK. The darkness of this time does not have to be your undoing. It is OK for you to feel frustrated, angry, let down, full of doubts. This is OK.')

This day in Sydney, in the midst of all my questions and doubts and wrestling, something stopped me on that street. Something inside. Feet slowed down as I came towards the old man. In the inner space there was a feeling that was becoming more and more familiar – an ache, a flame, a notion, an invitation. A whisper. A silent voice that told me I should stop my day and go and talk to the man.

Yet there was another voice, louder than the whisper. It stood up inside me and shouted protest and indignation. The voice of reason. The voice of social conditioning. The screaming defence of the Sculpted Self. It was a loud voice – the voice of fear, a voice defining who was safe and who was scary, who was worthwhile and who was not. 'Stranger danger' may keep our children safe, but it too often keeps us lonely. Joe was a lonely man.

The loud voice urged me to continue walking on into my busy day. It reminded me that this man would probably just want my money and rip me off, or spend it on alcohol or drugs. And what could I, some middle-class kid, say to an old man that would help anything anyway? The loud voice complained about the notion of a new action in my life. That was way too risky. 'Sure,' it seemed to say, 'you can have your cognitive and emotional faith crisis, but to actually change the way you live … come on … that is just taking it too far.'

On the pavement, standing awkwardly beside the homeless man, I found myself torn between the whisper and the loud voice. I was caught between the ache and the reasonable, the flame and the fear – between wanting to do something and wanting to just ignore it all. The coaxing of a new me, the safety of the old me. I could step out into uncharted territory or settle back into what was comfortable. Every journey begins with such a choice, the decision to leave behind the security of what has been, the fortress of our absolutes.

As I stood there looking down at the old man, another voice squeezed itself inside my already crowded head. This voice took its place between the whisper and the loud voice. It was a memory.

This memory was of the moments directly after washing dishes with the street worker. I was talking to the man who ran the drop-in centre. On the day I visited there were a number of extra volunteers, including myself, and I said to the social worker, 'You must be happy. A bunch more people to help out here.'

He looked back at me without a smile. 'Many come to view this place, Joel,' he lamented, 'but few ever stay. Many Christians seem attracted to the romantic notion of volunteerism and a mission to the broken world, until they discover how hard the work can be. They visit, but few do anything more about it.'

Not that I needed it, but this was just one more reason for me to get angry and frustrated and to rage against the tradition I had grown up in. Lots of moralistic talk, little action to bring about the betterment of the world.

I stood there by the old man, pretending to be looking at something nearby, and I realised that though I so desired to change my ways, I was also completely petrified of what that change might mean. Itchy feet and shaking knees. I was like the dog kept in a cage for many years. It learned to exercise by running around in circles, and when it was rescued and released into a big field, it still ran around in small circles. It was trapped in circles and so was I, running an invisible orbit in the midst of wide fields of freedom. The memory of captive living is so imprinted that it keeps us circling long after the walls are gone.

We have all become prisoners to our cages, captives to our fishbowls. We are so used to the cell of our fenced-in reality that the thought of the wide, open world is both exciting and terrifying. We have been forced to wear clothes that have become too small. We are locked into the story written for us by others, and their script is our prison. We have come to believe that the size and shape of the cell that holds us is the size and shape of reality.

However, on this day in Manly, to the surprise of all things conditioned inside me, I remembered the challenge of the manager of the drop-in-centre, steadied my courage and walked over to the old man. I offered to buy him breakfast. He mumbled that he had already eaten but pointed at the space next to him and asked me to sit down. I stepped out of my fishbowl, opened the cage door, broke the circle and sat at his table.

For the next hour I listened as he told me his life. He spoke of family and love and suffering. Many years filled with the bitter taste of sorrow. Dark times. A tale of loss. His wife and only child had been sideswiped and killed by a drunk driver. He was not a drunkard – had not touched the stuff since their death. He was not trying to swindle money out of me. He was simply an old, poor man slowly moving towards his end. An old man who … well … had a bad bed. He had a room in a Housing Commission block of flats a few suburbs to the north, and he was, in his words, 'waiting till the good Lord takes me home'. His mattress there was all but worthless, a thin strip of rubber that caused him sleepless nights and major back pain.

As we neared what would be the end of our conversation, I once again felt the flicker and the ache inside. This time it whispered that I should buy the man a new mattress. Once again the loud voice rose, screaming in protest, reminding me of all I could be doing with my hard-earned money. I hesitated, feeling again torn between what was and what could be …

~

How can we leave that which we have always known without some sense of loss? How can we leave those places deeply inscribed in our skin without a sense of pain and a tearing away from their comfort? How can we move our seat out from the kitchen table without a fond sadness for the memories so enmeshed within us? Such long hours were spent embedding what has always been us. We were held and carried by our sculptors' love and fear, their good intentions and broken actions, their comfort and pain. All this has worked its way under our skin and into our soul.

I am not just talking about the Western comfortability that I battled there on the street in Manly. I am not even just talking about privilege and entitlement. All of us face the inside battle over and over in our lives. The old us versus the new us. The whisper and the coaxing versus the loud voice of what has always shaped us.

We cannot leave that by which we have known life without a lament for all that it met within us. We cannot leave without a deep sense of regret and a fear and a sorrow. Even those hurtful stories, those painful pasts, as much as we may hate them, still cling to our identity. Too much of ourselves was made from these fragments. The memories have become our clothes, keeping us warm on cold nights.

Kahlil Gibran writes, 'It is not a garment I cast off this day, but a skin that I tear with my own hands. For to stay, though the hours burn in the night, is to freeze and crystallise and be bound in a mould.'[28]

Such is the pain and the necessity of unravelling, of moving forward. To stay is safety, to step out is danger and uncertainty. To stay is to be frozen, to walk forward is to be smashed in pieces and to melt slowly. But melting is the only way we can change our shape, the only way we can rearrange our frozen thought and existence. To stay is to lose ourselves, but to go on is to be skinned of our security, torn in two and unravelled at the edges. To shed the skin of the old.

The lobster too sheds its skin. It is the only way it can grow. It is a shedding that brings with it a newness, a rawness. We lay down our protective outer garments so we can live out of our fledgling selves. Raw and vulnerable and bursting forth into the new. Our frayed endings, our unravelled tendrils reach out to grasp that which is beyond them.

The Unravelled Self. A pioneer of what could be.

~

Once again, I tore myself from the grip of the loud voice, and I told the old man I was going to buy him a new mattress. He refused. I refused his refusal. He told me he didn't want to be a charity case. I told him that the very act of refusing meant he wasn't being one. I pressed. He finally gave me his address. I rang a bed company and arranged to have one delivered the next day.

The old man broke. Tears flowed from red eyes down dirty cheeks and into the forest on his chin. A deep, yellow-toothed smile of gratitude. I sat down and he hugged me. Fragile bones wrapped up in paper skin pressed hard against me. The smell of old sweat and unwashed clothes and stained memories. I closed my eyes.

I had never been hugged by God like this before.

God wrapped tight around me. I was in the arms of the Divine. God in the smell and the brittle bones and the weathered face and the yellowed teeth. God where I did not know I could meet him. God outside my fishbowl.

Our redemption always emerges from where we least expect it to come.

When we are willing to see the Divine in places we don't think he should be, where we have been told he does not play, with people we are sure he does not interact with, it is then that our eyes are opened. It is then that our fishbowl is smashed. It can hurt. It can cost us. Yet the freedom of the new frontier always outweighs the pain of our tearing.

So I shed my skin in his arms, I melted slowly, I tore away the clothes too small for my body. I thought of the words of the Christ, 'Whatever you do for the least of these, you do also for me.' On that day, I bought Jesus a bed. Not the sanitised, comfortable, Sunday-school Jesus I was used to, but the real Jesus. The gritty and dirty and smelly and homeless Jesus. I bought Jesus a bed, and in return he gave me a hug. And in this hug I heard a now familiar whisper, the soft voice, like a new friend.

There must be more than this.

In the arms of the old man, I felt God breath on the fires of my dissatisfaction.

There must be more than this.

I had let myself whisper these words at times in church and on my bed at home, and now I heard them in the silence of this divine hug.

There must be more than this.

I realised that I needed this man. Whether he needed me or not, I needed him.

There must be more than this.

I stood up from his embrace knowing that I was different. I had taken a first step out from the front door of my security, from all that I had known.

The crack had grown and the fishbowl had shattered, and I was leaving.

Leaving Home

You know that point in your life when you realise that the home you grew up in isn't really your home anymore? And all of a sudden, even though you have a place … the idea of 'home' is gone … It just kind of happens one day and it's gone. And you feel like you can never get it back. It's like you feel homesick for a place that doesn't even exist. But maybe it's like this rite of passage, you know? And you won't ever have that feeling again until you create a new idea of 'home' for yourself, for the family you start, for your kids. It's like this cycle … Maybe that's all a family really is: a group of people who miss the same imaginary place.

'Andrew Largeman' in *Garden State*[29]

The Pilgrims' Way

I write at the moment from my bed on the Holy Island of Lindisfarne, a small island in the very north of England. Snowflakes pelt against the window, smashed to sludge by the anger of the wind that howls around the island on a day like today. It whips up the ghosts of the past. In the 600s, a monastic order was founded here by the Celtic monk Saint Aidan. He had himself come from another community on another remote island, the island of Iona in the west of Scotland. The isolation of such far-flung places proved a magnet to these holy men who had left home.

The ground is blanket white outside, all the way to the edge of the surrounding sea. The paradox of snow on sand. I went out this morning. Never one to turn down the seduction of the wild wind, I walked around the island. I came to the place where its inner edge faces the mainland across a causeway. Lindisfarne is a tidal island; you can only get off or on it twice a day, when the water is called back out to sea. Every year, regardless of all the warning signs along the road, at least a few cars find themselves caught between the island and mainland England. Busy tourists trying to beat nature. Nature always wins. The helicopters come and rescue them.

Not far from the twice-a-day submerged road is a line of tall wooden poles. Before the road was built, this was the way out to the island. Thousands of pilgrims throughout the centuries have made their way along this line to Lindisfarne at low tide.

The Pilgrims' Way.

A few days ago, I walked the line of poles out to the island. Feet frozen, I had removed my shoes in my fervour to make it a memorable experience. To let the cold water wash some things away. To refresh my being in the world. A pilgrimage of my own.

The word *pilgrim* comes from the Latin word *peregrinus*, which means a person wandering the earth, an exile in search of a spiritual homeland. A pilgrimage is a journey through the physical world and at the same time a journey through the inner landscape. The heart of pilgrimage has always been to take a journey towards some sacred destination.

The pilgrims walked the path at their feet and they walked the path inside. The two were the same.

They came to these sparse locations at the edge of the world because they mirrored the journey of their spirituality. These were sacred places: the inhospitable wasteland away from the city centre; the landscape where silence and aloneness were their only companions. Remoteness, harshness, wildness. The margins. The desert.

Pilgrims are those who journey so that they may see differently. They are not the tourists who come to consume; rather, they allow their travels to consume them. They do not want knick-knacks but desire to reshape the very core of who they are. To wade into the depth of a place and let that place flow into the depth of the self. Sometimes we must wander around the edges to find what is truly at the centre.

The pilgrim journey perfectly reflects the Unravelled Self.

The pilgrim battles through the hard terrain and in turn is shaped by it. The quest to the outer limits reflects the quest to the inner limits. In the places of dislocation, all is stripped away. The pilgrim is awakened to a world that exists beyond their small self. They walk the path of questions and allow the journey to shake from them their habitual laziness, their rigidity. They wander, and in their wandering they are changed.

Traversing the forest that seemingly has no end. Ploughing through the scrub in the desperate search for what makes sense. Stepping out on the unbeaten path beyond the front door. A dissatisfaction with the unexamined ways of the Sculpted Self leads to the barren path.

It is the leaving of home.

~

Not all who wander are aimless. Especially not those who seek truth beyond tradition, beyond definition, beyond the image.
'Betty Warren' in *Mona Lisa Smile*[30]

A table split

In the emerging years between teenage life and adulthood, I found that many of the answers learned around the McKerrow kitchen table didn't quite fit where I felt they should. They did not flow as I felt they should flow. The confrontations of digging graves and meeting street workers and buying beds for strangers began to unpick something inside. A stitch loosened, threads pulled, ends frayed – and everything was up for debate.

At the table we learned the laws, ate the rules, drank the doctrines and mouthed the answers, but they were not enough for me anymore. Questions turned into disagreements. Absolute statements led to arguments. The McKerrow kitchen table was pushed back and forth, back and forth until … crack. The splitting of the table that had held all the answers.

All the answers, that is, for my dad. My dad, who also once cracked open his own father's table and spent years constructing the one we then sat around.

In those days of the cracked table, of the unravelling, I was like the whisper trying to find a voice. I was like the ant pondering the elephant that is God. Asking questions that would stop the world. Demanding that someone pay attention. I was incessant in my challenge and critique of a world that didn't make sense, a Christianity full of hypocrisy and a God who didn't fit neatly into what he was meant to.

I screamed my tantrums at this God – but now I see it was a God who looked a whole lot like my father, a God who looked like my church. My railing against the God of my youth was a railing against my church's and my parents' version of that God. Partly, this was the normal process of individuation. I was a teenager trying to find out who I was as a separate person from my parents. But I was also an emerging adult realising that God was much larger than I had been taught.

The table we sat around was not big enough to seat the One it was dedicated to. It could not contain the God who was always sneaking out from underneath cups of coffee and playing in sugar bowls of jelly and tipping over glasses and breaking rules and smashing dogmas.

This God was never a good dinner guest.

And so, in those days when I dined with this God, my father's table split in two. It cracked down its spine, splintering over questions without answers and the paradoxes of a God I could not see and yet could taste. The table broke.

~

At Christmas I had a rather violent argument with Pa, and feelings ran so high that Pa said it would be better if I left home. Well, it was said so decidedly that I actually left the same day. Things actually came to a head because I didn't go to church, and also said that if going to church was something forced and I had to go to church, I'd most certainly never go again, not even out of politeness … I was angrier than I ever remember being in my whole life, and I told Pa plainly that I found the whole system of that religion loathsome, and precisely because I dwelled on those things too much during a miserable time in my life. I don't want anything more to do with it, and have to guard against it as against something fatal.

Vincent van Gogh[31]

The disruption

In every life there comes that which calls us from the safety of home, that which cracks the table and splits it in two. We move our chairs out from beneath this broken table because we know we must. We walk out the front door and begin the journey because we know home no longer holds what it once did.

> We move forward because the old way crumbles under the weight of the new.
>
> We move forward because the hands that once held us can do so no longer.
>
> We move forward because we know what silence lies waiting should we remain.

Change comes to find us. We get hints of what could be, a whisper of something beyond our small stories. Sometimes it is a sneaking suspicion that all is not as it should be. Sometimes it is a storm and a flash of lightning, a thunder which shakes the very foundations. The unravelling may come as an awakening or it may come as a dying, a freedom or a fracturing.

Either way, it comes always as a disruption.

> An invitation.
>
> A scent on the wind.
>
> An inciting incident.

In narrative theory, this is what such confrontational and revelatory experiences are called: 'inciting incidents'.[32] They are the things that move the story forward. And they are as real in life as they are in novels. The experiences that cause us to stumble, to open our eyes and look around, as though coming awake from a long sleep. The events that set everything in motion.

A wizard draws a mark on the round door of a Hobbit's home.

A light smashes on the ground at the feet of Truman.

A rabbit runs past Alice.

Neo takes the red pill.

Hagrid arrives on a stormy island after Harry's letters are intercepted.

Katniss's sister is chosen during the Reaping.

Charlie finds a golden ticket.

For me, it was

the digging of a grave.

standing at a kitchen sink.

buying a bed.

the incongruence of my beliefs and actions.

the taste of something without knowing its name.

the reality of my past.

the dreaming of a new future.

the inconsistencies of the people around me.

the deep knowing that there must be more.

the baby bird stepping out of the nest.

the foreign smell carried across the shore.

the constriction of the world that was.

the new world that lay waiting.

For others, it may be

a new learning that resonates when the old teachings feel shallow.

an experience of God that feels as though you walked into heaven itself, only to then have your closest not really understand, or want to.

a book that your community told you to steer away from, but when you nervously opened the first few pages it felt like someone finally understood who you were.

a writer who speaks of what you have never heard, or what you have always known but never had the words for.

the passionate fire you feel inside but do not see in the lives of others.

the university lecturer who challenges what you were taught to be truth.

your life when it did not go the way you were told it would.

the death of a loved one, or a love that leaves.

a partner who has been raised around a table so different from your own.

a church that has given itself to the game of politics.

a church leader who tells you how you must vote.

a whole tradition that has come to look more like a political party.

Sometimes the fire has gone and you wake up one day to realise that the passion has left.

Sometimes it is the contradictions and disagreements that arise in what has been one's nurturing community.

Sometimes it is the contradictions found in the self.

Sometimes it is the simple feeling of not fitting.

Sometimes it is illness and suffering and sorrow.

Sometimes it is sexuality.

Sometimes it is nothing more than absolute frustration at the state of the world.

Sometimes it is nothing more than absolute frustration at the state of your own heart.

The inciting incident may feel glorious or it may feel like a nightmare. Whatever it is, it means things can no longer remain the same. These whispers, these storms, these urgings ignite the fires of our dislocation. The locale for all that we have known is no longer there.

The Unravelled Self is the place of exile.

A university lecturer once told me that every change begins with a dissatisfaction. This dissatisfaction is the threshold, that which moves someone from the safety of the Sculpted to the wilderness of the Unravelled. It disrupts the normal flow and stability and sets you on a different path.

Those who begin the journey soon move from these niggling dissatisfactions into larger explorations. For beyond the front door lie the mountains and the mystery. We move into the wilderness of the question, the arid lands between the fertile. In this sparse landscape, it is the uncertainties that are our great transformers. Here in the desert, here in the in-between, we discover who we truly are. This desert, as Richard Rohr says, 'is the ultimate teachable space.'[33]

~

To believe in God or in a guiding force because someone tells you to is the height of stupidity. We are given senses to receive our information with. With our own eyes we see, and with our skin we feel. With our intelligence, it is intended that we understand. But each person must puzzle it out for himself or herself.

Sophy Burnham[34]

The dark night

For some, the journey of unravelling leads to adventure. A new world to be explored. The sunrise of hope after a claustrophobic night. It is a stretching of limb and a feeling of unfolding.

For many it is the opposite. The unravelling is painful. They are pushed from behind, not embraced by the open arms of invitation. Over the cliff they fall, grabbing for something, anything, to stop the chaos, to make them feel normal. They plummet, tumbling and dizzy. They are lost. Everything taken.

The Unravelled Self may be the dark night eternal – or seemingly eternal. It is the autumn and the winter season. A shedding. A sadness that looks like a storm. The mother standing by the grave of her son. The lady lathering soap to wash away the unwanted touch. The old man and his frailty. The young man and his failure.

When the unravelling arrives, it can knock the breath and the words from our lips. There are some things too painful for naming. They leave us silent in the grief of what we cannot speak. They are too much to bear, the last straw upon a back weighed down. The cruelty of the world and the God who was meant to love us.

In this tempest of pain we can only hold on, and barely even that.

In 2015 a friend of mine had twins, one of them drastically sick. She spent most of his first year with him in hospital. On New Year's Day 2016, he stopped breathing. The ambulance came, rushed him again to the hospital, kept him alive. She told me, 'It's hard to know where to go with these experiences.' I wholeheartedly agreed. There are often no words in a time of unravelling. These things are too heavy for naming.

Another friend lost her daughter 25 years ago. She still carries around her absence. The absence has become more familiar to her than her daughter's presence. My own parents lost two children, twins, right after they were born. It was not something we talked about growing up. Too heavy.

I shall never forget the phone call to tell me that my first high-school love, only a few months before her wedding, had suddenly and inexplicably died in the night. I was a wedding photographer back then and had three weddings to shoot that week. The camera was the heaviest it has ever been.

~

Besides death there are other things too heavy for naming.

Like unwanted touch.

Like keeping his secret.

Like blade on wrist on tiled floor.

Like slamming the door.

Like the drop of your stomach when you are found out.

Like the drop of your stomach when you find them out.

Like the silent emptiness that fills a space once all the people and laughter have left.

Like the crippling feeling that no matter what you do, it is never enough.

Like the shame you just can't quite name.

Like the loneliness that comes after a night on social media.

Like bruised eye hidden under dark glasses.

These things too are a loss and a grieving, and most often we do not have the language to speak of them. So where do we go with them? When pain surges in upon the storm, when the dark visits, when our shoulders bow under its weight – where do we go with all that is not right?

Usually I run to the water. Moving water. When nothing makes sense anymore, I turn to the ocean and the river. I have found that grief is a grindstone, and so is the ocean. They break us apart. They rough away the sharp and the piercing. They smooth us out, even as we hide in their depths.

So I let myself sink under the water and stretch out my lungs beneath the spray. I surrender. I let myself be smashed. The wave breaks and turns and tosses and smooths me down. And on the beach I pick up the pieces, sea-glass green.

In our society we are trained to run away from such sorrow. We are told that self-comfort is the way to happiness. We go to a place of coping, of numbing. We do all we can to not fall apart. Batten down the hatches. Tape up the windows. A bottle in one hand, shopping bags in the other. Chocolate and ice-cream, computer games and isolation. Or never letting ourselves be alone. Whatever it takes to escape. Good or bad, healthy or self-destructive, we cope, for we cannot see a way through.

Pain, too, is a baptism. Perhaps, in the end, they are one and the same sacrament. Pain and baptism. They are both a loss of breath and a dying, a drowning that leans towards beginning again.

The ocean decides when it is finished with us. It gives us back to the world of men. On the beaches is where we pick up the pieces. Smashed now, made smooth.

I am not saying that this is the answer or the cure, to place yourself in running water. I am not saying that there *is* an answer or a cure. As much as we demand it, the unravelled is seldom something to be cured. What I am saying is that the swirling ocean is as good a place as any to hide – to hide like a grain of sand, like a piece of smashed glass.

In other words, I am saying that the only place of healing I have found is to enfold myself into the arms of something much larger than myself. To abide in the place of unanswered pain. To not run from it back into cliché and the safety of absolutes, but to let the wild ocean have its way.

Some say we should turn to God in such moments of despair. And I guess this is my way of doing so. The ocean. God. Enfolding my own story of that which cannot be named in the hands of a larger story. Weight held by weight, like my son lets my hand hold his hand.

~

> Please pray specially for me that I may not spoil His work and that Our Lord may show Himself – for there is such terrible darkness within me, as if everything was dead. It has been like this more or less from the time I started 'the work'. Ask Our Lord to give me courage.
>
> **Mother Teresa[35]**

~

I do not know what this looks like for you. I do not claim to know where you should go with these experiences, this weight. The disappointment. The unresolved. I only know my own attempts to pry gripping fingers away so that I can let something out as surrender into the ocean. Into God. Not holding the grief back but giving myself to the waters so that they might someday smooth me out. Shattered glass turned sea-glass green. On the beaches is where we pick up the pieces.

Pain is a wave that breaks over us, a freedom and a fear. The dark night is the moment when we let go of our control. I have never known the freedom of the breaking wave without the fear of what it is that it may break. It is the surge of our becoming. It is the whisper of our future. It is the building of our love. It calls us beyond ourselves, to be let down into the water as death and pain and to somehow rise again.

And what for you? Could there be a new beginning? A resurrection? The gold only ever purified by the furnace? The strength that flows from deep weakness? Could the dark night be the womb of a new morning? The winter that holds deep within it the emergence of spring? The little seed that stretches towards the sky, still buried deep in the soil?

We hold on to this hope, though for now, in the unravelling, it is so very hard to see.

The Unravelled Self walks along a path that does not seem to end. The way of descent, the way of not knowing. We have left the surety of self, or have been shoved forcefully from it. We are raging. We are alone. We are unravelling.

Flailing wings in the midst of a world that no longer makes sense.

~

So you mustn't be frightened, dear Mr. Kappus, if a sadness rises in front of you, larger than any you have ever seen; if an anxiety, like light and cloud-shadows, moves over your hands and over everything you do. You must realize that something is happening to you, that life has not forgotten you, that it holds you in its hand and will not let you fall.

Rainer Maria Rilke[36]

Leaving Society

Man, I see in Fight Club the strongest and smartest men who've ever lived. I see all this potential, and I see squandering ... an entire generation pumping gas, waiting tables; slaves with white collars. Advertising has us chasing cars and clothes, working jobs we hate so we can buy s— we don't need. We're the middle children of history, man. No purpose or place. We have no Great War. No Great Depression. Our Great War is a spiritual war ... our Great Depression is our lives. We've all been raised on television to believe that one day we'd all be millionaires, and movie gods, and rock stars. But we won't. And we're slowly learning that fact.

'Tyler Durden' in *Fight Club*[37]

Expectations and accusations

The world does not make sense. At least, not anymore. Not like it did when I was a child and the world happened around me and I didn't have to look too closely.

Our hyper-consumerist society does not make sense – this way we play out our being-together. I once thought it normal, but I cannot accept it as normal any longer. I have left it behind. Well, at least I have tried to, with varying degrees of success. I have seen the fishbowl for what is, an oasis with a price. A fake reality that promises everything yet costs us and the world so much more than it delivers.

We bring the values of this consumerist, Western Dream fishbowl into relationships. People simply become objects for consumption, things to satisfy our needs, stuff to be used and tossed away. We bring these values into our self-perception and see ourselves as broken products, replaceable and non-unique. It is the commodification of self and others at the expense of our personhood.

We bring these values into our spirituality. We pray to a self-serving, vending-machine, instant-gratification god who is supposed to 'show up' in our lives. It is what John Drane calls 'The McDonaldization of our spirituality.'[38]

We bring these values into our dreams for the future, upholding a fake reality and expectation of what life is meant to look like.

This hyper-real consumer fishbowl has created some hugely problematic expectations in the lives of the fish swimming in it. The Western Dream is as seductive as it is costly, but the seduction is made up of empty promises. We feel the letdown because our expectations are never met, but we don't know who to blame.

Expectations of what success *should* appear like. Expectations of what romantic relationships *should* feel like. Expectations of what sexual experience *should* be like. Expectations of our physicality and what our bodies *should* look like. Expectations of what our gender *should* be like in this world. Expectations of God and how he *should* manifest in our lives. Expectations of what the Bible *should* give to us when we open it up. Expectations of what church *should* do for us. Expectations of ourselves and what our lives *should* be like.

Friends, *should* is an ugly word. The reality is that life will not work out the way you thought it would, or the way you felt you were promised it should. You have held on to a version of success that will not come about.

There is only one place these false expectations can take us … disappointment.

Disappointment in success. Disappointment in romance. Disappointment in sexual experience. Disappointment in our bodies and our gender. Disappointment in God and how he was meant show up in our lives. Disappointment in the Bible when it doesn't give us our quick-fix answers. Disappointment in church when it doesn't live up to the standard we set for it. Disappointment in ourselves.

The question is, what do we do when our expectations are betrayed? What do we do with our disappointments? Who do we blame?

Who do you blame when you felt sure you would end up married but are still single?

Who do you blame when your marriage is not what you were promised it would be if you did all the right things?

Who do you blame when a loved one dies too soon?

Who do you blame when your career fizzles into debt?

Who do you blame when life does not work out the way it was meant to?

Most of the time, we blame God. We also blame our church, or our family, or whatever our sculpting community has been. We blame anyone and anything except our own expectations.

Many people have this idea that God is meant to provide for them what they ask in the way they desire. When God doesn't come through in the way they expect, they end up throwing God out entirely.

The Unravelled Self spends a lot of time pointing accusatory fingers.

~

Coupled with this expectancy is a notion that the lifestyle you have right now is not enough, that it doesn't reach the standard. So you chase and chase after it but cannot reach it, and you are left believing that you are not enough.

Friend, this too is untrue, but this is exactly where our society wants you. Where it *needs* you. A society based on economic growth requires us all to keep consuming. Being someone who feels they are not enough, who is disappointed and anxious, is exactly what advertisers want you to be, for it means you will buy more of their stuff to alleviate those feelings.

Those who promise the world through their product also want to turn our attention away from the origin of these products. We do not know where our food is harvested. We do not know where the plastics that make up our toys come from. We do not know who puts together our computers and how much they are paid for it. We do not know who picks our coffee beans. We do not know.[39] Very few of us sit down to think about the people further down the line – those who pay the price for us to have our cheap clothes and cheap phones and cheap coffee.

We have a suspicion that someone, somewhere, is going without due to the affluence in our lives, but mostly we ignore this feeling. The media does a thorough job of blacking out our fishbowl walls. The glitz and glamour of consumption stops us seeing the world as it is. All this *stuff* allows us to separate ourselves from the reality of a broken world – the reality of a daughter slaving away for $2 a day, a farmer starving, a brother picking waste out of rubbish heaps. We live in a world of illusion. The hyper-consumption fishbowl allows us to live in lavish wealth and prosperity and still feel like paupers.

In this disastrous system, no matter what we have, we will always desire more, and no matter what this desire is for, it will never be fulfilled. It can't be. Otherwise we would stop purchasing products and experiences, and our economically driven society would crumble. So we must be kept in perpetual self-disdain, with the carrot of wealth, fame, belonging and acceptance held out just in front of us. If you are miserable, stressed and anxious, if you forever feel like you are inadequate, if you just want to fit in, then you are ideal for the economic growth of our society.[40]

The Unravelled leave the societal values they have known, for they feel that something is wrong with this world, and they feel a profound sadness at this wrongness. A sponsor child advert on TV, watching a movie, an article on Facebook, walking past a beggar on the street: whatever inequality they see, it eats at them. They feel a deep-seated guilt at perpetuating a world so highly unfair. They are outraged that they could have been duped by this system, and rightly so.

~

I sit on a man's back, choking him and making him carry me, and yet assure myself and others that I am very sorry for him and wish to ease his lot by all possible means ... except by getting off his back.

Leo Tolstoy[41]

Who is our neighbour?

In the Christian Scriptures, we hardly ever see the person of Jesus directly answering questions. To most questioners he gives not answers, but more questions. Larger questions. Better questions. Questions to send them on a quest. He told parables with open-ended interpretations. Jesus was a master at moving people forward from their Sculpted Selves into the unknown of the Unravelled.

The teaching form of the *parable* lay at the heart of this movement. It was the same as the Buddhist Zen masters' use of the *koan*. The parable, like the koan, was a paradoxical story, a riddle used to provoke a response. It aimed to bring about movement, to lead people down a certain track of conventional thought and then throw in the hand grenade.

The well-known parable of the Good Samaritan does exactly this, though we miss its impact due to our familiarity with the story. The parable is not just about being nice to your neighbour as is conventionally thought. Let's have a closer look …

The story is told by Jesus to a powerful man, an expert in the law, who asks him a question. 'Teacher,' he says, 'what must I do to inherit eternal life?' (Luke 10:25).

Now, when you read the words 'eternal life' here, please don't jump to the common modern understanding of this term: that it refers to a place called heaven where people go when they die. This was not the understanding of the phrase at that time. It is our Western, fishbowl-tinted lenses that read the text this way. Rather, we must try to understand what the term meant for those at the time.

The New Testament Scriptures were written in Greek, and when we look at the original Greek, we find that the words translated 'eternal life' in the English Scriptures are the words *zoe aionion*. These can literally be translated 'life of the ages.' The man wasn't asking Jesus how to go to heaven when he died. Rather, he was

> asking about the new world that God is going to usher in, the new era of justice, peace, and freedom God has promised his people … there is no sense that this 'age to come' is 'eternal' in the sense of being outside

space, time, and matter. Far from it. The ancient Jews were creational monotheists. For them, God's great future purpose was not to rescue people out of the world, but to rescue the world itself, people included, from its present state of corruption and decay.[42]

This story is not about some other-worldly existence one might call heaven. It is about heaven being a reality on earth. It is about a society of peace and justice. It is societal. It is economic. It is political. It is about God's dream for the world.

The story continues with Jesus posing a question back to the Questioner:

> 'What is written in the Law?' he replied. 'How do you read it?'
>
> He answered, '"Love the Lord your God with all your heart and with all your soul and with all your strength and with all your mind"; and, "Love your neighbour as yourself."'
>
> 'You have answered correctly,' Jesus replied. 'Do this and you will live.'
>
> But he wanted to justify himself, so he asked Jesus, 'And who is my neighbour?' (Luke 10:26–29).

Jesus then tells the Good Samaritan parable to this lawyer and to those around. The story is of a Jewish man robbed and left for dead on the side of the road. Two other Jewish religious men, those whom you would expect to help, ignore the man and walk to the other side of the road to pass him. What we don't think about is the fact that the people Jesus is directing this story to, including the lawyer, are exactly these sorts of men – the religious elite, the powerful.

Jesus comes near to the end of the story and throws the punch. The pious and powerful Jewish religious leaders may have walked past the man, but a Samaritan man, a member of a people group despised by the Jews, stops and takes care of the beaten Jewish man. This Samaritan is someone that Jesus' Jewish audience would have hated. They would not have expected such a plot twist. Jesus was not telling a story just about being nice; he was directly stirring and challenging his hearers. He was laying a hammer to their fishbowl. He was directly challenging their prejudice and calling their elitist system into question.

Perhaps today, instead of telling the story of 'The Good Samaritan' to the Jewish elite, he would tell the story of 'The Good Muslim' to right-wing conservative Christians. 'The Good Pro-choicer' to a group of pro-lifers. 'The Good Donald Trump Supporter' to a group of left-wing socialists. 'The Good Black Man' to white supremacists. 'The Good Gay Man' to Westboro Baptist ('God Hates Fags') Church. The 'Good Asylum Seeker' to a group passionate about border protection.

What story would he tell you? Who do you neglect in the elitism of your fishbowl?

The parable was a sucker punch. It was in their face and screaming. It was not teaching to give answers but teaching to create larger questions, questions that would evoke a response.

The easy answer is too often an anaesthetic that numbs the hunger. On the other hand, the parable, the koan, the question, is as salt on the tongue of the hearer. It makes them thirsty. The clichéd answer holds us back from true knowing. True learning is only born of wrestling and doubt and struggle. True learning can only come through first unlearning, unravelling. We must empty ourselves of our staunch absolutes and our prejudice towards our Samaritans.

The expert in the law is not the only one who wants to justify himself regarding how he treats those around him who are different. I have done this throughout my life. Insisting that I am righteous. Insisting that I live fairly. Insisting that I am not sexist, for sexist people abuse women and talk down to them. Insisting that I am not racist, for racist people wear pointy white hats and tell Muslims they are evil. All that is not me. I have not personally done anything wrong.

But I am more than just me, more than just an individual. I am not separate from wider social reality. Whether I realise it or not, whether I like it or not, I am one with humanity. The good and the bad all flows through me. I am part of a system that perpetuates gender discrimination and I am part of a system that perpetuates inequality and I am part of a system that perpetuates racism.

I am a perpetrator. Crossing to the other side of the road and ignoring the beaten man while claiming we are living in a post-racial society. This is colour-blindness born of a colour-blind system.

I need to look no further than my own land of Australia, with its history of colonisation leading to genocide. The slaughtering of the masses in the name of God and Britain. And it is not just in our history. The constitution of Australia does not recognise Aboriginal and Torres Strait Islanders as the first peoples of Australia and it does not protect their rights. Australia has the worst life expectancy of Indigenous peoples in the world, with a UN report showing that Indigenous Australians are dying up to 20 years earlier than non-Indigenous.[43] Indigenous children aged between five and 17 die from suicide at five times the rate of non-Indigenous children.[44] Of all those Indigenous Australians who have committed suicide, nearly 100 percent were people living below the poverty line.[45] Around 50 percent of Indigenous Australians aged 15–64 are unemployed.[46] The national rate of imprisonment of Indigenous people is 15 times higher than non-Indigenous. In Darwin's prisons, Indigenous men make up 98 percent of inmates. An Aboriginal teen is more likely to go to jail than go to high school.[47]

Indigenous Australians are refugees in their homeland. Racial inequalities abound, and yet still the average Australian sees no problem with the way things are. Post-racial society indeed.

There is a wound in this nation. It bleeds. When you are not looking, it bleeds. When you turn away, it bleeds. Red blood from black skin. Yet still we seek to justify our reality. Still we have the audacity to ask, 'Who is our neighbour?'

It is time to leave, to let the illusions crack and fragment. It is time to cross the road towards whoever it is lying beaten in the street. It is time to stop hiding ourselves away in the societal pockets of comfortability. It is time to challenge the systems that perpetuate such disastrous inequality.

The Unravelled challenge the systems they have been caught up in for so long. They see them for what they are. They rage against their prejudice. They refuse to see individuals as one-dimensional. They refuse to see the problem as merely individual.

~

When I feed the poor, they call me a saint. When I ask why the poor have no food, they call me a communist.

Dom Helder Camara[48]

95

Leaving Faith

The house church splits, and it creates two craggy cliffs. I am on neither one of them ... I read a verse aloud mechanically, but I can't hear my own voice. I am there. I am not there. I am gone, disappeared, lost entirely to the in-between. I am a grey particle, floating. I am drifting into the void ... I am falling. I am dead weight, and there is no one to catch me ... My answers are complicated, filled with questions, filled with doubt and frustration. They run out of the spaces and into the margins ... I don't have the language to articulate the growing darkness I feel. I don't know why I am sad, only that I can't seek to shake myself out of it ... Every Thursday at morning Bible study, I have been pouring less milk from the bearded man's cardboard carton into my coffee mug. By April, I am drinking it straight black. Black and rich and bitter. Black like truth. Black like reality. By April, I am ready to leave the Church People.

Addie Zierman[49]

Preaching to the masses

I walked slowly up the side stairs and onto the stage. A few breaths and it would be my turn to speak. The lights were shining bright and blinding. The mic invited. I could just make out the masses of people clapping their hands before me as I walked to centre stage.

The auditorium was filled with thousands and thousands of young people from churches all over the area, and it was me who stood now on stage to inspire them. I was 21 and filled with nervous energy. Never had I spoken to this many people before. But this is what I had always wanted – the dreams of a younger Joel to be a mega-church youth pastor preaching to thousands in auditoriums.

It was not long after taking that early morning walk and buying a bed for Joe that I joined the staff at the church where I grew up. Being one of the passionate, 'on fire' young people in the church ensured me a spot on the youth ministry team as a youth leader, and when school finished, a youth ministry intern. Then, when the previous youth pastor left, I was given the job. And now here I was, a few months in. The packed-out auditorium. The accolades of being a 21-year-old who would be asked to speak at an event like this. The growing youth ministry. This had been my dream. Some want to be a firefighter; I wanted to be a pastor. Specifically, a mega-church pastor. Speaking truth to the masses. Leading the revivals.

The problem was that I no longer felt a part of this world. Of course, I wanted the podium; which passionate and charismatic 21-year-old wouldn't want the opportunity to speak to so many? But I didn't fit anymore. The songs that had been sung before I took to the stage made me cringe. The prayers that had been prayed and the masses of 'Amens!' accompanying them, the excited young Christian teenagers jumping up and down at the front of the stage – all I could see was the shallowness of it all. The consumer Christianity. The many wanting to be fed but not living out a radical life of serving the poor and marginalised as Jesus told us to. How I judged these people I was just about to speak to.

I realised the extent of my dissatisfaction with this whole scene the moment I became the youth pastor I had dreamed of becoming.

My church had spent the previous few years raising money for a new building. The old building was replaced by a contemporary auditorium with all the lights and speakers you could ever need. A few million dollars later, with people re-mortgaging their houses to give to the project, the new building was ready. The congregation now gathered in air-conditioned bliss. It was high fives and celebrations and praise-the-Lords.

And I just couldn't do it.

A waste of money. A waste of resources. A waste of time. I thought of the many who needed the money to survive. I thought of the beds that could be bought. Our money had built church buildings while beggars were still on the street. We didn't need air-conditioning; we needed to get up off the pews and actually do something.

I was unravelling from the church world that had held me throughout my youth. I could see all its insufficiencies, all its hypocrisy. I was leaving 'The Faith' I had known. I didn't know yet if that meant I was leaving Christianity, for I was getting more and more passionate about following this Jesus I was discovering and more and more disappointed and angry at the church.

My fire didn't leave me during this time of unravelling. That came during a later great unstitching. No, I was as passionate as always. But by this time, I was not passionate about the fishbowl. I was raging against it. The irony was not lost on me that now here I was speaking at this massive church rally. My dream of being a mega-church youth pastor had become a reality. I had three interns working under me, 50 youth leaders, a few hundred teenagers and a brand-new building to do it all in. The problem was that I didn't want it anymore. Not if it meant the teenagers weren't getting out there, out of their Christian bubbles, out of their comfortability, out of the building.

While I was pushing people out of the building, the other church ministers were trying to get people into it. Every Tuesday during staff meeting I was asked for the youth ministry numbers from that weekend. How many young people had come to our programs. If the numbers were down, I was questioned as to why.

I hated those numbers. I hated those meetings.

So I started my own. A church inside my church. A small group of young people who were also sick of the domestication and sanitisation of the radical Jesus. They were as dissatisfied as I was and willing to question and challenge. They were just beginning to open their eyes to the reality of the world.

We would gather together and look at the Jesus of the Scriptures and the Jesus of our church, and bemoan how far apart they were. The two seemed to be polar opposites. They were black and white – we certainly could not see the grey back then. *I* certainly could not see the grey back then.

We thirsted for new ideas and bigger understandings, with a deep knowing that *there must be more than this*. We read books from outside our tradition. We were chasing autonomy and accepted each other for where we were at. Yet at the same time none of us were willing to simply throw out the tradition that had sculpted us, as constricted as we felt by it. We questioned, we challenged and we sought to live differently. We threw ourselves, in all the passion of emerging adulthood, into whatever new, exciting thing was speaking to us at the time.

We didn't do any of it well, but we did it passionately. Sometimes we were too rebellious; perhaps sometimes not rebellious enough. Always agitated and full of fervour. It was a small, radical group pursuing something more amid the sausage factory that was our mega-church. That is how we saw things anyway.

So with my outrage bursting forth and my zeal to bolster me, I stood on stage in that youth rally and opened my mouth. And I told them this night was a total waste. I am sure this is not what the organisers who had worked so hard and believed so much for this rally expected me to say. I am sure this is not what the pastors of my church expected me to say. But I kept going. It was a waste if we young people didn't leave from this night and get involved in the community around us, if we didn't change our lifestyles. It was all a waste. What was the point of praying for our city if we were not willing to go and be a part of the lives of the people who lived in it?

For my Scripture that night I used every rebellious youth pastor's favourite.

> I hate, I despise your religious festivals;
> your assemblies are a stench to me.
> Even though you bring me burnt offerings and grain offerings,
> I will not accept them.
> Though you bring choice fellowship offerings,
> I will have no regard for them.
> Away with the noise of your songs!
> I will not listen to the music of your harps.
> But let justice roll on like a river,
> righteousness like a never-failing stream! (Amos 5:21–24).

I went hard at them. I challenged and rebuked and gave them a zealous, passionate exposition of what I felt they needed to hear. I talked about the outrageous Jesus. I told them they were not following him. I called them hypocrites and told them they had started following another gospel. I felt righteous in my indignation. I went over my time limit. I did not care, so zealous was I to smash apart their fishbowls.

Indeed, the Unravelled easily become just as arrogant and judgemental as the Sculpted. It was not that such a message was not what they needed to hear. It was that it is hard to listen to someone as self-righteous as I was, as I can still be.

Needless to say, it didn't work. I am not sure what I expected to happen. Perhaps for all the combined churches gathered there to be so moved they would stand up and unanimously agree to sell all their buildings and start community centres across the region. A revival of a different kind. Whatever it was, it did not take place.

What did happen: to start with, I was not asked back again. I was told by people that they thought I was advocating too much of a 'social gospel'. I was reined in by the senior pastors of my church.

All of these things only stoked the fires of my righteous anger towards these nurturing communities of my sculpted faith. My unravelling was as discriminatory as my sculpted reality. There was no grace there. I pointed the finger of accusation. I judged the hypocrisy. I certainly didn't want to be called a Christian anymore. I would call myself a Jesus follower, but not a Christian.

What I had not realised through it all was that my rebellion was still so closely linked to my desire for affirmation, my desire to succeed. The performance mentality that had so shaped my evangelicalism now shaped my resistance. I would be known as so passionate that I had to go the way of the radical. The rebel.

I have seen many of those unravelling, including myself, walk around with the badge of rebellion, unorthodoxy and progressivism pinned proudly to their chest. Yet beneath my chest there was still the same cry,

'Look at me. Somebody, please, look at me.'

The absence of God

I could still feel God back then, even in the midst of the unravelling and questioning. Even as I questioned my whole Christian upbringing, God was still close. And today it is not that I can no longer sense God. But it is different. I am different. God is different.

For starters, I try to refer to God as a *she* just as much as a *he* these days. I am not sure my old church would approve. But isn't all our language about God only ever metaphor, including our gendered pronouns? Words to articulate something that can never be articulated. Verbal words used to refer to something far beyond language.

The words are not reality. They are more like symbols. They bridge between our contextual understanding and the fathomless reality that is God. They give us a language, a way to dive into the depthless mystery whose ground is God. Not my definition of God. Not your definition of God. Rather, a mystery that is larger than any definition.

To us, God is both known and unknown – at one and the same time as close as our skin and as far away as the Moon on some other planet on some other day. We may know God, but only through glasses, thick with lenses, embedded with colours, painted from the years of our own understanding. We are in bondage to these things we think we know. The answers we hold so dearly are just another notch on the belt of our own insecurity.

The Sculpted Self insists that God look like THIS. The Unravelled Self, however, insists that God is *not* THIS. The time of unravelling is a breaking down of the fences of delineation, of what is and isn't. A smashing of the walls to live in the freedom of being fenceless.

Since my early teens I had felt God, or what I perceived to be God, standing right beside me. Always. A closeness that was without description. An intimacy. A breath. A person. It was always there. She was always there. I could close my eyes and find in moments that space where I felt I was in the very presence of the Divine.

It began when I was 13. Alone in my bedroom, praying, I had an experience of God. A presence came in the room. A benevolent presence, full of love and power. My whole body began to shake. Suddenly my feet were swept out from under me and I found myself on my back, in my room, speaking a different language. Babbling sounds out of my mouth. Strange, I know, although if you are in the charismatic/Pentecostal tradition of Christianity you may not think it strange at all. In these traditions this experience is called 'speaking in tongues' or 'baptism in the Spirit'. Whatever it is called, it may actually be part of the very thing you are unravelling from.

But for a good Anglican boy this was a baffling experience. It was an invasion from totally outside my fishbowl. I thought I may have gone crazy (some of you probably think I did). But it was a mystical experience that changed my life. It stirred in me a fire so bright that it birthed the passionate Jesus Freak of my teenage years. It brought about an earlier unravelling, a teen move away from the conservatism of my church and into the wild world of the Holy Spirit and the charismatics. I was desperate for God, weeping tears of unrestrained zeal. God was alive and I was his biggest fan, and it was doubly delicious that it was so different to the world I had known.

This experience was my first real breakaway from the faith of my parents and my church, my first unravelling from what I thought to be true. The presence of God followed me closely throughout the following years.

But if I was familiar with God's presence, there are many who are much more familiar with God's absence. Especially during the unravelling. God is not then as close as the skin but far, far away. God once seemed intimate, and with such intimacy came the expectation that it would always feel the same. That God would always be.

Until God was not.

Until he disappeared.

Unless it was, in fact, we who disappeared. For this feels much the same as God disappearing. It is just easier to blame the invisible one for leaving than to blame ourselves. At least it was for me, just a few short years later, after preaching to the masses at the auditorium. Let me tell you about it.

~

In my case, as everything else was dying, my faith seemed to die, too. God had been there. God had been alive to me. And then, it seemed, nothing was alive – not even God ... My faith bristled; it brittled; it snapped, like a bone, like a pot too long in the kiln ... I had been a person who felt God, who felt God's company; now I was becoming a person who wondered if I had dreamed up God, and then a person who was tired of her own wondering ... You wonder if you have invented the whole thing: maybe it is not God has removed himself from you; maybe simpler, there is no God. You tell yourself you have evolved, maturing past needing a god. You narrow your eyes at your absent God the way you would narrow your eyes at a lover, in a fight, when he has just said something awful and mean and true about you, the way you narrow your eyes before you say Fine then! and storm out of the room.

Lauren Winner[50]

~

The day you learn you can hurt people is a dark day indeed. Inside and out. There are many people I have hurt and disappointed over the years. Friendships stretched, assumptions made, communication faulty. The knight with rescuer tendencies in shattered armour. The loss of centre in the gravitational pull of another's brokenness. The giving too much of oneself. The rains of misunderstanding.

I lay broken on the floor all that week, the week I hurt those closest to me. The week I realised I had been hurting all those closest to me for some time. That week ripped the blindfold off, one I had been wearing without realising it. In a relationship that had become co-dependent and unhealthy, the co-dependence was named and outed for what it was. The cycle of enmeshment. The entwining together of too much shadow. Too much given and too much taken.

We both said sorry at the end, and she left. I have seen her very few times since. I, the rescuer, and she who could not be rescued. Not by me. Not by anyone but herself.

It is amazing how one can lose oneself without realising it. It is amazing how one can lose God without realising it. It is like taking step after step after step and then looking back to see only a mark on the horizon.

I lay on the floor all that week feeling the sinking blackness of having betrayed those I loved. Having betrayed myself. Having betrayed my calling. I felt small, ashamed – ashamed that I would lose sight of the finish line, ashamed that good intention could be coated so thickly in darkness, ashamed that what I most loved in this world, to journey alongside, had become the very thing that crippled me.

That same week was when my first girlfriend, mentioned in an earlier chapter, died in her sleep. Yet as a wedding photographer I still had three weddings to shoot in a week. It was one of the worst weeks of my life. It was the smallest I have ever been.

I lay on the loungeroom floor, foetal. I would get up and shoot photos at a wedding and then go back to the foetal position. The next day, shoot a wedding again, then come back home and lie foetal once more. Interestingly, those wedding photos were some of the best I ever took.

At the very end of the week I had a vision. An image in my mind that named the reality of what was.

I saw myself riding armoured with sword and breastplate and shield. I saw myself falling. I saw myself flailing. I saw the Divine hand that reached towards me. Fingers pressed into my chest, pierced the chest armour and then pierced flesh, all the way through to heart cavity. Then came the tearing apart, chest cracked down the centre to open the cave inside that held my heart. It was barely beating, covered in thick ash and hardened black.

When the veil is torn away, aren't we all crumble and fracture somewhere inside? Aren't we all shadow? Aren't we all barely beating heart and sorrow?

The hand reached in, took my heart and held it tight. And then slowly – so slowly – the hand began to pump. The ash fell away, the hard coating peeled back. The thick red of life was still in there, somewhere deep. The heart began to find its beat in the hand. The blood began to flow, and the final piece of black cracked off. And as it did, I screamed. Not just in the vision in my head; I lay on the floor of my lounge room and screamed. The piercing cry of an arrow-bled hawk. It echoed around the house and out into the forest around. It echoed back to my ears, and in it I heard a freedom. I felt a freedom.

I had not realised I had lost my freedom, not until that moment. I had not realised how much of myself I had lost. I had not realised I had indeed become a barely beating heart. My passion was gone, my fire extinguished. I didn't know who I was anymore. My God had been left behind, the one who for so long had been so close. I cannot pinpoint when, but somewhere back along the track I had stopped talking to him. I had stopped listening to him. I had stopped attending to him.

I had stopped listening to myself. I had stopped attending to myself.

This was not the unravelling of systematics or dogma or theology. This was the unravelling of soul and presence and self and purpose and intimacy and the very experience of God. This was a leaving without realising I had left. A loss of faith in God.

And a loss of faith in self. After all, wasn't I the one who was going to change the world? Wasn't I the passionate one and the radical one and the gifted one and the one with the big heart and … now I could hardly get up off the floor.

But I did. Slowly.

With the little strength I had, I pushed myself up from the ground. I stumbled towards a mirror and looked my broken self in the eye. I could not look God in the eye, not then. I tried to say sorry to the stranger looking back at me. I punched the mirror instead. Thankfully it did not smash.

I was the one who had been smashed that week. A million pieces and scattered. I had lost my form and my definition. But the hint of the whisper of the freedom that came after my scream on that lounge room floor – this was what I desired. Desired. I had a desire. Freedom. To come back to wholeness. The smallest slither of a hope.

It would take a long time to collect up all the pieces of me, and a lot longer to see them put back together. Not as before, but as something new. Something mosaic. The beauty that may come from the ugly.

~

What do you do in the midst of this absence? Where do you go? What do you try? I try all kinds of things, all my old tricks for getting through – I try anxiety, I try bourbon. I pray. I don't pray. I go to church; I keep going back to church. I make myself busy, so that I don't have to look at the wall. There is boredom here, and loneliness; there are also Eucharists and angels. God darts by; sometimes I notice.

Lauren Winner[51]

Eating pizza

My friend Rowan has grey hair these days. The silver fox. When we first started coming alongside emerging adults in their times of unravelling, his hair was brown. I wonder at the correlation. We have been doing this for a long time now. He has also just completed his doctorate (or near to it, depending on the date this book is published) and has three children. These things may also have had some impact on his hair colour.

Rowan tells the story of running a group for teenagers at the church where he was leading. The young people were the core, committed types who were very active in the programs of the church. They were also the ones who had grown up within the church, and so in times of teaching and discussion these students would always give the 'right answers'.

Rowan felt this was just a cursory giving of the 'right answers' rather than a genuine expression of what the students thought and where they were actually at in their lives. The 'right answers' were a shallow response and a way to avoid the harder truths that run deeper than just being correct.

One night, instead of a formal time of teaching and questions, they just sat around and ate pizza. One of the leaders sitting with them spoke up and asked the question, 'If your faith were a pizza, what kind of pizza would it be?'

The group laughed at the odd question but then actually began to think about it. How do you give the 'right answer' to that kind of question?

There is no 'right answer'. It was a question that required more of them.

One brave person broke the silence by saying that her faith would be a Capricciosa. It may not be a Super-Supreme like Mother Teresa, but she was comfortable with where she was at.

Another person declared that theirs was a Mexican pizza because they were so fired-up about life.

Another girl then courageously said, 'My faith would be a Hawaiian pizza.' This was met by laughter and a hail of abuse as earlier she had spoken of how pineapple should never, ever be used on pizza. But she stood her ground and responded, 'That is my point. I say this because pineapple should never be found on a pizza, and I know there is stuff in my life that contradicts my beliefs. Stuff that doesn't belong there.' The group went silent.

There it was. The deeper truth. A cracking of the surface to talk about reality, about truth, all by talking about pizza. The 'right answers' did not matter so much anymore. As Rowan reflected, 'The bravado of a correctly answered question and triumphal expressions of faith had been replaced by vulnerability.'

Another of the students took courage from the girl's honesty and responded by kicking an empty pizza box across the floor and saying that his faith was just like that box. Empty. Where there once was something delicious, nothing remained, just the smell.

The group had moved into new territory together. Real stories were truly being told through the metaphor of pizza toppings. It gave the students a way to interpret their reality and articulate their story. To be vulnerable together. To admit that beneath the surface of 'the right answers' there was a chaos of questions and wrestlings and struggles and doubts.

The way of doubt is as holy a journey as the way of faith may be. Doubt is never the opposite of faith; it is its very building block. Faith can only exist in the midst of doubt. Certainty, on the other hand, leaves no room for faith.

The telling of the students' stories broke through the shallow shell of answers and invoked from them a true response, a vulnerability, an authenticity.

The hardest thing we ever have to do is open our lives, give ourselves in the screaming face of our isolation.

Truth be told, I have found this beneath-the-surface reality in every single community I have been part of. It is always there in one way or another. There is a mess just below the surface of all our lives. We can either ignore it or choose to name it.

The problem is that such authenticity, such genuine vulnerability, is not seen or encouraged in most churches, nor in other institutions in our society. We stay on the surface level, and so faith also stays on the surface level. It doesn't penetrate through the masks we wear into the darker spaces inside where there might be nothing more than the smell of a pizza long gone.

The problem is that often these kind of responses from people are not held well. They are dismissed or shouted down by Bible verses and cliché, by what we claim is truth.

However, the stories told by these young people were a truth deeper than proposition, deeper than logical rationality, deeper than doctrine – deeper than the right answer.

Leaving Truth

Every fact of science was once damned. Every invention considered impossible. Every discovery was a nervous shock to some orthodoxy. Every artistic innovation was denounced as fraud and folly. The entire web of culture and 'progress,' everything on earth that is man-made and not given to us by nature, is the concrete manifestation of some man's refusal to bow to Authority. We would own no more, know no more, and be no more than the first ape-like hominids if it were not for the rebellious, the recalcitrant and the intransigent.

Robert Anton Wilson[52]

Mowing the lawn

One of the more hated chores of my childhood was mowing our back lawn. Our house was on the side of a hill, a hill that looked more like a cliff, especially on mowing days. To make matters more complicated, my dad owned a Flymo, an electric mower that ran like a hovercraft but meant you had a 40-metre trail of cord behind you as you navigated the backyard cliff face. You had to puzzle out a route and make sure you didn't accidentally run over the cord. It was a little like a live version of the snake game on an old mobile phone, except an electric shock greeted you if you ran over this tail.

One day, as the grass cutting was near completion, the smell of fresh clippings filling my nostrils, the small boy who had just moved in next door quietly approached. I saw him out of the corner of my eye. He had a quizzical look on his face, staring down at the mower. He held his breath, as if the contraption in front of him may suddenly disappear.

He yelled above the rumble of the mower, 'What are you doing?'

I turned it off.

'What are you doing?' he repeated in the humming silence after the noise had ceased.

I thought it was obvious, but responded in truth, 'Ahh … I'm mowing.'

He looked back at the mower, doubtful. 'No, you're not. That's not a mower.'

'What do you mean?' I responded. 'Of course it is.'

The little boy said again, 'No, it's not.'

I was not sure why I was arguing with this little boy, but I asked him, 'Why do you say that?'

'Well,' he replied, 'a mower has four wheels and that doesn't have any. And a mower doesn't have a cord like that. It doesn't run on electricity. It runs on petrol. My dad has a mower and it doesn't look anything like that. You're not mowing, so what are you doing?'

For five minutes we debated. I tried to explain that just because it didn't look like his *dad's* mower didn't mean it wasn't a mower. I told him to look behind me and see the results of my work. The grass had been cut. The mowing had been done. Hence, this was a mower.

You could see his little brain bulging at the concept. He had never seen an electric mower before and yet here was this thing cutting the grass. He looked up at me, a hint of new understanding.

'If you say so.'

He rolled his eyes and walked away.

~

The circle was a circle
until I walked around the corner.
The square to stay a square
until she walked around my own.

The powers that be built a wall upon our street.
    Between the buildings and the factories
    Between the circles and the squares
    Between I am right and you are wrong.
They built a wall and we threw our stones.
I threw my stones till she asked me
    to walk around the corner
    cross the wall that stood between us.

I stood
where she had always
looked up upon my circle
to blink in disbelief to see
it was a square.

The next day
she came to where I had always made my home.
She turned to her square, she saw it as my circle.

From the shapes that we believe in
to the God of three dimensions
our angles
do betray us
until we walk around the corner.[53]

~

Truth is much larger than I first thought. While we try to jam triangle shapes through circular holes to quantify our world, the spiritual things of life seem to avoid this sort of universal definition.

From my perspective God looks like a square; from your perspective God looks like a circle. We can either go our separate ways and stay none the wiser, or we can turn the corner, walk around the wall and come face-to-face with the cylinder that is the Divine. A three-dimensional plane that opens out into our two-dimensional spirituality.

How easy it would be if we could call God a square and all our ideas about him were nice-fitting right angles. Alas, life does not seem to go that way with things beyond the scientific. We do not live in a black-and-white world. We live in a world of mystery and paradox and colour. Bright colour. Soft colour. Harsh colour. Colour born of the light we humans cannot see: ultraviolet, infrared, x-rays, radio waves, gamma rays. A whole world we cannot see. And how much more so the spiritual realities around us. What we perceive is a sliver of what is happening.

How humbling. How I am forced to admit that my ability to comprehend Truth is so finite.

111

The movement into the Unravelled is a movement of unlearning. It is a letting go of the models of reality that you might have insisted were the only True reality. Mowers. Three-dimensional shapes. Colour spectrums. Light waves. There is always more than the individual eye can see. What has fit so neatly together now no longer seems so clear cut. The Unravelled is a time of searching for, questioning and wrestling with what might be truth. It is disjointed and dislocated, incoherent and fragmented. A flung-wide multiplicity.

The Unravelled Self is the stage of deconstruction. We rip apart the maps that were written for us. We move away from the undulations of who we are *meant* to be, what we are *meant* to believe. We sift and take apart. We crave clarity in the midst of the murky. The things we have held so firmly become the very things that hold us back. Our knowing gets in the way, and once unalterable beliefs begin to flex and bend under the weight of questions and inconsistencies.

The Unravelled is the stage where you desperately want an answer and at the same time rage when someone tries to give you one. Between doubt and hope there seems no place to land.

With this time of sorting out and throwing out and experimenting with comes the realisation that the Divine can never be caught. That God can never be contained inside our absolutes. That doctrine is only ever theory mixed with experience. We come to see that our attempts to put a box around God and define her are like a blind man describing the sunset. Or perhaps, like a seeing man refusing the experience of the blind.

Our definitions are always too small. We need a change of perspective.

Am I saying that there is no such thing as absolute Truth? No. I just do not think that we can ever fully ascertain what that Truth is. We will always fall short. We will always be ants pondering the elephant. A grain of sand on the infinite shore that is God. The truth that we come to know is only ever 'in part'. It is only known through the coloured lens of our own experience.

But what *does* get us closer towards Truth, what gives us a greater understanding, is always our ability to listen well to the other.

A man named Glen once said to me, 'Tradition betrays you when it is not flexible – when it is not challenged by other people's traditions.'

Those who challenge our ways of thinking, our bias, our ingrained patterns, our fishbowls – they are a gift. If we are willing to receive. If we are willing to lay down our need to be right all the time, to be in control. If we will hold ourselves loosely in the face of others, not speak in absolutes, not be so defensive. If we will let their thoughts rub up against our own. This is how we move forward. This is how we get rid of the boxes we squash God into. We look to the margins, to the periphery. We look away from the script that has always been and learn a different story.

The Unravelled Self is all about questioning what you thought you knew. Our inner world changes when we allow our thoughts a spaciousness we have not given them before.

Psychologists call this neuroplasticity – the changing of our cognitive world. It is the ability of neurons at their synapses (the points where they connect and pass on the electrical signals in our brain) to forge new connections. To break away from their traditional patterning and be rewired. The patterns in our brain can find new ways of coming together. Things can change.

The Unravelling brings about a repatterning of our perspectives. An open-handed holding of categories emerges as we allow others to tell us what they notice about our fishbowls. We listen to those who speak from the periphery and we change. God looks very different through the eyes of a poor mother in West Papua than he looks through my own. But is this not a beautiful thing? We may learn from each other and so grow in our perspectives.

To leave what we have always named as Truth is to come to the edge of our knowing and take a leap into unknowing. Our growth comes in the realisation of how much we do not know. We unlearn our absolutes. We return to the child state of discovery where there are no experts. Zen Buddhism would call this the 'beginner's mind'. Jesus named it having faith as a child.

~

A Zen koan from Japan tells the story of a university professor who came to a Zen master to ask him about Zen. The Zen master served him tea. He poured his visitor's cup full and then kept pouring. The professor watched the overflow until he could no longer restrain himself. 'It is overfull. No more will go in!' 'Like this cup,' the Zen master said, 'you are full of all of your own opinions and speculations. How can I teach you Zen unless you first empty your cup?'[54]

The posture of your questioning

Sometimes the right questions can help us more than the right answers. Sometimes there is no answer, just the question and the process.

The answers we have given to each other in the painful moments, the uncomfortable moments when life does not make sense, have more often been for our own security in the face of the vast unknown. Clichéd answers, neat and tidy answers, *right* answers, show themselves as a shallow form of response when it comes to the deeper complexities of life. When it comes to the sorrow and the mystery. We are frightened of a world we cannot contain and a depth we cannot manage. In our fear, we box everything up into nice, tidy and contained systems of answers. They are our attempts to compartmentalise our world to keep it under control.

The invitation towards the Unravelled, though, is something completely different from control. The invitation is to recognise that it is neither the destination nor the answers that will move us forward, but rather the journey itself. The invitation recognises that the very point of the questions is not to find the answers but to let the questions shape who we are. The true destination is our formation through this process.

By this, we are changed in ways that knowing the answers would never accomplish.

We run too quickly into solving. We run far from the way the wild winds would blow us. We douse the flames before the unanswerable fire forges us. We would rather hide in the safety of the answer than sit in the tension of the question. But I urge you, give focus to the unresolved things. The ache. The niggling that lingers in the forgotten places of your inner life. The pain of unanswered problems and the uncertainty of mystery. Give focus to the deconstruction – not for the sake of tearing apart and criticism, but to discover the parts that held your world together in the first place.

The invitation is not to latch onto answers but to live the questions. Let them bubble up out of your inquisitive being and point you forward. Each of us is heading somewhere – whether we want it or not, our lives are on a trajectory towards who it is we are becoming. There is no way to be rid of this reality. We are caught up in its flow, pushed from behind and pulled from ahead. We are not a static people.

The questions stand out before us as stepping stones on the path. We, so eager for the answers, look too far to the horizon and so miss the steps at our feet. We panic because the edge of the world looks so far from us and we cannot see the way through. We are stuck before we even start; we do not move. We claim that we do not need to move because we know the answers already.

Yet if we turn our heads down … down … down to the stepping-stone questions, we will see that every place we want to end up is made up of many, many steps.

The question is an open door. A threshold to an entirely new world. An invitation to a quest. Do not stare too far into the distance and feel overwhelmed. Rather, look to just the very next step and take that one. The one after that will come into focus and then the next and the next. The steps will come together, and soon you will realise that you are living as the person you so desire to become. The journey the questions placed you on was the answer all along. The answer was, in fact, your very life being lived out.

The first question. Let it move you. Let it become the first step for your journey.

~

What is your first question?

Right now, what is the question that is bubbling up in your life? The one you may have resisted for far too long? It may be a scary question to ask, but ask it anyway. You may not trust where it will lead you; ask

115

it anyway. Whatever resistance you feel, ask it anyway. Risk it. See what happens. Ask it not to answer it but with a different intention. Ask the question to wonder at it.

'To wonder' is a very different posture from 'to answer'. Wondering evokes openness. Awe. It does not seek to shrink the world down into digestible units but to widen things. Wonderment is a freeing motion. It celebrates mystery. As we look at the world through the eyes of wonder, it is then that we see more wonderful things. Such a posture flows into the very essence of our being, as the way we *see* in the world becomes the way we *be* in the world.

The Sufi poet Rumi writes, 'Observe the wonders as they occur around you. Don't claim them. Feel the artistry moving through, and be silent. Or say, "I cannot praise you as you should be praised. Such words are infinitely beyond my understanding."'[55]

It is this sense of wonder that separates cynicism from true questioning. The cynic asks questions to make the world smaller. The wonderer asks questions to make the world larger. The cynic shuts things down. The wonderer opens things up. The great challenge of the Unravelled Self is to not lose the wonder in the face of all you could be cynical about.

It is no surprise that many of the great spiritual traditions uphold the transformation that happens through this wondering. The questions, the uncertainties, hold us as clay to sculpting hands. They call us beyond our own capabilities and understandings. The quest that the question sets us on changes everything, for it changes us.

Writer and story theorist Donald Miller suggests that this personal transformation is actually the whole point of a story. It is not the epic tale that makes a story great but the transformation of the protagonist, the arc of the main character. When we see this main character develop and transform, that is when we come away satisfied from the story.

He writes, 'If the character doesn't change, the story hasn't happened yet. And, if story is derived from real life, if story is just a condensed version of life, then life itself may be designed to change us, so that we evolve from one kind of person to another.'[56]

If the reality is that in life we run too quickly to the answers, perhaps it is the wisdom of the Divine that in regard to the deep things no answer is given. The Divine would rather that we change than know the answers. Ours is a story of character transformation rather than a short flight into fancy.

So hold the questions within. Let them do what they are meant to do: free us from ourselves and set us on the truest of quests – that of self-transformation.

~

> The quest for certainty blocks the search for meaning. Uncertainty is the very condition to impel man to unfold his powers.
>
> **Erich Fromm**[57]

Pitfalls on both sides

There are many ways to not make it through the wilderness of the Unravelled. Quicksand and avalanche. Deserts too dry and poisonous vipers and mountain trolls (or, even worse, becoming an internet troll). There are ways to walk the path well and ways to never make it out alive. There are also many ways to help people take the journey, and many ways to hinder their trek. Here are some examples.

1. Throwing out the baby

We too easily throw the baby of faith out with the bathwater of whatever cultural Christianity we have known. We discard all the beliefs and practices of our sculpting community out of retaliation and trying to throw off the pain, out of rebellion and what we perceive to be freedom.

Having fused together the spiritual journey with the culture and beliefs of our sculpting community, separating faith from cultural Christianity may for us be the most important part of the Unravelling.

Be it the passionate teenager who sees the hypocrisy in his church or the single mother who believed her life would be different, the back door has been flung wide open. In the Christian faith in the West this is clearly seen as research shows around 60 percent of young people in the USA who have grown up in the faith end up throwing it all out by the time they are 24 years of age.[58] It is decidedly easier to toss out one's sculpted belief system entirely than to sift through and wrestle. We run away from the old rather than see it transformed.

When the beliefs of our parents aren't large enough, we do not delve into them to find how they may be re-used; we discard them. When church doctrine is too small, we get rid of the church. When religion is too hypocritical, we toss it. We too easily leave rather than refine. In our questioning and in the face of hypocrisy and small-mindedness, we throw out the totality of our beliefs and replace them with a bland notion of ... *whatever feels good.*

I put it to you that we are more than this. That *you* are more than this. By throwing out all the old, we don't actually do the true work of the Unravelled Self. We divorce ourselves from the learning space of tension. It is far easier to not call myself a Christian than to still do so while thoroughly shaking up, challenging and questioning the Christianity I am a part of. Far easier to not listen well, to simply run the other way.

In our criticism we forget that our past has been so needed in our growth. We forget that the old deserves to be honoured, even as it is questioned and reworked and reconfigured. We forget that we need it still, only transformed.

There are those who during this time simply need to throw God out. But in fact they are not throwing God out at all. They are merely throwing out the God of their upbringing. The challenge is then to keep searching, to keep on the trail.

2. The arrogant critic

Another great danger of the Unravelled Self is getting stuck in its wilderness. We can lose ourselves, not in the socialisation of the sculpted, but in a world deconstructed, with no hope of reconstruction. Lost in the desert. It is a bitter end.

'Bitter' is the right word. The embittered. It is an easy trap. The

Unravelled Self births the antagonistic sceptic and the spiteful, hostile and belligerent critic. When a frustration towards those who see the world in black and white is coupled with an arrogance, there comes the critic. When one listens well to new ideas but not to the people who have gone before, to the guidance of the old traditions, there comes the critic. When there is a willingness to challenge the system but not to challenge the self, there comes the critic.

Critics see the faults in others but never in the self. Or perhaps they see the faults in themselves and lash out at others in their self-hatred. Either way, they refuse the helping hand. They hold the world to ransom for their disappointment. The arrogant critic is the shadow side of the Unravelling Self – a person who becomes stuck in their dissent. Their journey of growth becomes even more immobile than that of those they criticise. The Unravelled journey is often a lonely one, yet I have never met a lonelier person than the arrogant, bitter critic.

The selfishness of arrogant rebellion and 'playing the victim' is a close cousin to the feeling of being misunderstood. Too often in their wake comes the breakdown of relationship. Friendships are fractured. Resentment festers. Questions turn to a deep-seated scepticism, a selfish pursuit and a carelessness about consequence. Fathers leave families. Mothers walk out the door in search of what they think they are missing. People stop talking to each other.

For too many, the world becomes smaller rather than larger. Their pride gets in the way of true searching. The smashing of other people's fishbowls becomes an ego-driven pastime.

However, the things of subversion and wrestling and questioning do not have to be accompanied by arrogance and cynicism. There will always be relationship tension, but it does not have to bring about a breakage.

To those unravelling, I urge you: guard yourself against that which tastes bitter. The nasty. The cruel. The biting. If there is a sure way to get stuck in quicksand, this is it. Indignation slopes down into an angry nihilism and a wretched spitefulness and a disgruntled resentment. No wonder the sculpting communities of many feel betrayed and judged and misunderstood by those who are separating from them.

An unhealthy unravelling allows outrage to turn into arrogance. A healthy unravelling chooses to turn outrage into actions – to allow dissatisfaction to reshape one's lifestyle.

One of my students, after hearing a lecture on societal realities, went home and labelled all the food in the pantry and fridge that did not come from an ethical source. He then proceeded to tear apart his parents for their buying habits and challenge them that if they were true followers of Jesus they would ...

These is the reactions of the Unravelled. So much passion realised in such a short time demands they *must* do something, anything, about it. Everyone else around them can instantly seem slack in the light of these great social causes they have now stumbled on. They cannot believe how selfish everyone in their nurturing communities has been, how uncaring and unthinking.

Too easily the Unravelled Self becomes just as arrogant as the Sculpted Self can be. Too easily the Unravelled Self becomes the angry activist. Such a person forgets the very reason they are standing against the system in the first place. They become so consumed with what they are standing against that they forget what they are standing for. The Unravelled Self defiantly knows what it is opposed to, but it can forget what it is called to.

3. Non-tolerance

The Unravelled can be someone so hurt by their sculpting community that they do not realise they can easily hurt them back. At this point neither ends up feeling listened to. Both feel betrayed.

The Unravelled Self is a time of profound miscommunication, both from those unravelling and those they are unravelling from. The old nurturers often do not know how to walk alongside a person during their days of unravelling. They fear the mess and the loss of control. Unravelling is a breaking out from the external rules and expectations previously placed on a person, and this is a form of existence with great risk. It is often not tolerated, especially when it comes to a church's HOT BUTTON issues.

Name any of them and I will be able to name the many, many unravelling young people in the church setting who question the conservative church's stance around these issues. And sadly, I have not met many young unravelling people who are listened to and supported and encouraged in this questioning by their church, even if their elders hold a different opinion. I *have*, however, met many young unravelling people who end up walking away from the church and their faith because they were not given the space to journey through these things.

In the Dr Seuss movie *Horton Hears a Who!*, an elephant named Horton thinks he has heard a minuscule creature on a small budding flower. He begins to ponder that possibly there is a whole world on this flower that needs his help. By his questions, he challenges the current way of seeing the world held by his fellow animals. He tries to convince others of this new 'small people theory' but very soon comes up against the authority of the Sour Kangaroo. Horton tries to convince her that reality may in fact be more than we can see or touch, but she does not want to hear it. She tells him he must stop telling people about his absurd theory. In her words, such thinking 'is just not something we do or tolerate here in the Jungle of Nool.'[59]

Many voices will speak in opposition to the Unravelled. Some will come down hard with claims of authority and what is in and who is out, like the Sour Kangaroo. Others will apply a more subtle pressure, whispering of 'weirdness' or 'strangeness' or 'falling away' or 'back-sliding'. Such whisperings bring about a slow but sure sense of rejection. The result is a walking away, not a falling away: a choice to – often understandably – leave the community the unravelling person is already implicitly estranged from.

Whether it is the Sour Kangaroo's declaration of non-tolerance or a whispering isolation, the effect is the same. Deep-seated abandonment.

My prayer is that sculpting communities and their leaders learn to hold the unravelling person with an open hand and a graciousness, regardless of the communities' own opinion. To listen well to their story. To create a safe space where that story can be told. To not demand adherence but to offer total acceptance. To allow space for their different conclusions. To name what is happening for them so they do not feel like a heretic, a washout. For the leaders to tell the truth of their own painful reality. For them to simply be present to the unravelling in their time of disturbance, not seeking to 'bring them back into line' but supporting them in their explorations. To model a healthy way to walk through the desert, and to help them get up again when they fall there. To let them walk out onto the limbs where all is not safe. It takes a profound courage and humility to let people do this, even if you think they will fall.

I hear the response to these words coming back: 'But there is Truth and we need to stick to that Truth so we don't end up all wishy washy and liberal.'

If this is the defensive posture that comes up in you as you read these words, then you are missing my point. My point is that people matter, that relationship matters, *so* much more than your understanding of Truth. We miss the spirit of the law because we are so focused on the letter of the law. The spirit of the law is always love. Jesus boiled all the commandments down to two: love God, love others. That was it. A love with no conditions, no standards placed on what someone must believe or how they must act.

I can also hear the defence coming up: 'But Jesus told the woman caught in adultery to go and sin no more.' Yes, he did. After he cleared the temple by saying, 'He who has no sin be the first to cast a stone at her.' They all left. We too would all have left. None of us perfect. All of us hypocrites. Today we use this story as a justification for condemning others' lifestyles and totally miss the point. The point is about unequivocal acceptance.

No condemnation. Always and always, unconditional love.

4. Love the sinner, hate the sin

One of the most quoted clichés in the church world around our hot-button issues is 'Love the sinner, hate the sin.' I wish this statement could be thrown out of the church's lexicon. We don't use it when we talk about the hoarding of wealth in the church or about the idolatry of nationalism (I wonder why not?). It is reserved solely for those hot-button moral issues. It is a statement that reads like a 'but', as in, 'I love you, but ...' The 'but' is a condition. A standard. Another way to make an *us versus them*. I will love you up to a point and then I will judge your particular sins as worse than my own, and I will call this 'loving the sinner.'

How horrendous it would be to go up to an overweight person and say, 'I love you, but I hate your fatness.' We all know there are many psychological, nutritional, metabolic and physiological reasons why someone is obese. It is not as simple as saying they are gluttonous and gluttony is a sin. How indecent to think so. How would this person feel if they were told this?

Now transfer this to any other issue that you feel like quoting the 'love the sinner' cliché at. The reality is that such a statement or anything like it does not and will not bring about a safe place for the Unravelled to continue in their journey. It is not a statement of love. All the Unravelled hear is the silent but screaming *but*. Spoken straight from the lips of a people they once called their own.

What I see in the Scriptures is more in line with 'Love the sinner, hate your own sin.'

Actually, I wouldn't even hold to that. I would say instead: Love Jeremy, or Sarah, or Frank, or Lisa. Don't strip someone of who they individually are and label them 'sinner'. This is not the heartbeat of their identity; this is not the name God gave them. Call them by their name and love them as a nuanced, complicated, intriguing, beloved, whole person.

And then, do the same for yourself. Love and forgive yourself. And in so doing, begin to see the brokenness inside yourself, the brokenness that causes what you call 'sin', transformed.

Love and forgive. Always.

A true community of loving acceptance. Can you imagine it?

This is what the church is meant to be. Could be. Sometimes is.

I have such hope in the church and what she is meant to be, for I have seen communities that embody this. I have been part of church communities that embody this. I am a member of a local church community in Melbourne that embodies this. It is a beautiful thing to be part of.

5. Going it alone

The Unravelled too easily throw everything and everyone away. But it will take community to help you get through this. True community.

If you are from the Christian tradition, it takes a church that can help you walk the rocky path. Or if the church you are part of does not help you, there will be people within the church who may. Look for them. Talk to them. Be honest with them. When you find these people, when you come to know your tribe, do not let go of them. Sometimes this is the only thing that will get you through the desert.

To those unravelling: I assure you, there are those who are trying. Those who *want* to try. There are people in your sculpting community who desperately love you and want the best for you. Their heart is good, even if they don't know how to express that in ways you can receive right now. Too often these good-intentioned ones are met with the cold shoulder from those unravelling. There is a refusal to engage and dialogue.

Of course, sometimes such a refusal is needed, especially in the case of physical, verbal, spiritual or cultural abuse. And I am definitely not suggesting you stay in such relationships.

But when this is not the case, when there may be room for relational connection, I urge you: as you ask the hard questions, and as you discover and wonder and challenge and deconstruct, stay connected. Do not simply walk away.

When there is no one to help us navigate a path through the desert, we end up getting stuck in our unravelled cynicism and bitter arrogance. The Unravelled need a guide, a desert instructor. Not someone with all the answers. Not a tour guide. Perhaps more a Sherpa: a mountain guide who knows the terrain, who can help you read the weather, who can carry your burdens for a time, who can point the way and accompany you on the journey – but who also lets you walk out that journey.

It is a choice for the Unravelled to walk in humility and recognise that they need others to lean on. It's a choice to not be governed by their ego in this. When everything else has slipped away, there should be a hand to hold in the walk across the desert.

Who is going there with you?

Who will allow you the space to wander and hold out their hand of support when you fall?

Who will sit in the midst of the pain and not seek to rescue you?

Who will not try to answer all your questions?

Who will remind you to keep walking?

Whoever this person is, choose them. Show them the unravelled threads of your existence. Allow them in. Be honest. It may be the very thing you need to keep walking forward.

It is OK

Lastly, and most importantly, to my friends who are unravelling, I want to say to you: may this book be some kind of permission slip for you. Permission to be where you are at. May you know that you are not alone, that there are many, many just like you. May you know that it is OK – that *you* are OK.

No matter what seems to be falling apart within you, no matter how far you feel you have walked away from what was, you can give yourself permission to be in this space. To not fear it. To walk away from the shame and guilt and judgement that chases at your heels.

It is OK for you to doubt and wrestle and struggle.

It is OK for the passion you once had to morph into a different shape, or to not be there at all.

It is OK for you to ask questions and experiment and discover, and to screw it all up as you go. All of life is a tension to be managed, not a problem to be solved. You may fall too far into critique and rebellion for a time; you may blend too far into conformity for a time. But wherever you are at, all of this is … OK.

It is the necessary act of reassembling who you were into who you are becoming. A faith rearranged so that it is not your parents' or your church's or your friends'. It is yours. This rearrangement, this reconstruction, is the beginnings of what we might call a Woven Self.

Search

They say that a girl who,
walks the edges of this world
will find herself,
if she looks for long enough.

But to see the beauty of may be,
she must turn her face from what was.
Unravel yesterdays
and the ways these ropes
would bind her,
the familiar city streets that held her
as a baby become a child, a child become a lady.

But maybe this cityscape has held you for far too long.

So wriggle your toes a little,
crack the clay,
stretch your fingers,
let them point you in the right direction.
Move your limbs, until you forget.
Do not look back with longing.
Your longing should always
face the direction your feet are pointing.

I still see sweet dreams of melodies
play through your head.
Take these notes and
lay they out on the ground before you, a path,
through the mountains, through the cold and beyond.
To the valleys, where frozen arteries are thawed,

the summer sun of promises come.
The pastures of river and spring,
the desert and the wilderness.
The ocean.

Break free now, my lady. Search the edges.
Swing wide the narrow gate, walk fast the narrow path.
Slip flowers into the spokes on bicycle wheel.
Hike up the edging of your skirt, run the wind.
They say that a girl who
walks the edges of this world
will find herself,
if she looks for long enough.

I see the journey has been long.
Spatters and splatters upon your fading dress. Limp of leg.
You are pilgrim. You are done. Exhausted.

The wind wraps its finger around you.
The sand between bone and sinew.
Turn now your face
into the harsh breath of the wind.
Let it burn away. Let it scrape away.
Let it sculpt your face as sandpaper to stone.
It is better to walk blind than fall back to sleep.

If there were another way around this mountain,
you could run the world in such shorter days.
But the souls who have gone before, they never found such a way.
They walked this path of pain,
they wrapped it around their wrist.

But if your wrist is too small,
then would you wrap it around your God.

He is the one who made the mountain in the first.
Lift up your skirts, run the river tide,
your faith is more than just air in the sky.
It is flesh. It is blood. It is mud. It is mire.

So run, like 50 tonnes of shattered memories are not enough
to hold you down, run like you were falling,
run like the spider's legs are not enough, run like a stallion,
run like your world is just about to begin.

And here, in this new day, sometimes the sky will still be grey,
but every day, somewhere in this world,
the sky is always orange and yellow and purple and gold.
So let's chase sunsets together,
like we've never seen them before.
'Cause if we catch enough of them,
maybe the grey skies won't matter so much anymore.

Walk the path, run the valley, crawl the desert, cross the ocean, climb
the mountain
until you come home, until you come home,
until you come home,
into the soft arms of who you have always been.

Part 3:
The Woven Self

A Boat Story (continued)

The boy was given a boat. A wooden boat. A small boat for a small boy. The storm had landed and the boy had held onto that boat until he could do so no longer. From the mast of the boat he tied a rope around his waist and he let the boat hold on to him.

He thought he would drown. He just about gave up all hope.

Until, without him even realising, the storm began to let up. It did not happen all at once, but at some point the boy noticed the waves were not so mountainous anymore. The wind was not so wild. Little by little it eased until he sat there, shivering, crying, tied to a broken boat. He wished his dad was there to find him.

The wooden boat was beaten. Battered. Shredded.
Surely beyond repair, yet somehow, still afloat.

The boy looked down to see water was leaking inside fast. One of the planks had been torn away by the waves. So the boy did the only thing he could think of. He pulled off a loose piece of wood from what had been the railing of the boat and snapped it in half. Just the right size. He jammed it tight into the hole. The water slowed to a trickle.

He inspected the rest of the boat. The sail was torn, dangling limp and useless. The rudder gone. More holes in the hull, more water leaking in. Ropes snapped. The mast broken in two. One oar gone. The boat was a disaster. Un-sailable. Highly sinkable. At any moment it felt like something would give and it would all just fall apart.

Way out there in the ocean there was nowhere he could dock his boat and repair, but he knew he had to fix it somehow or it would be over. He was lost and alone. Everything he knew, gone.

Just a small boat on the wide expanse of an unfamiliar sea.

Then he heard a noise. Something over the edge, bumping against the boat.

He looked over the side and saw a piece of driftwood. He picked it up. A little further on he saw another, this time larger. A wooden plank. It was the perfect size for a makeshift oar. So now he had a pair. He looked over the edge again and saw around him many floating things. The flotsam and jetsam of other boats and shipwrecks and rubbish dumped at sea. The storm must have swept it all into the same currents as it had him.

He found some more wood to use as a rudder. More rope to tie his boat back together. Fishing line to thread the sail. He prised out useless parts of his boat and reworked them into things he needed. The seat he tore off to make a mast. One more loose railing became a boom for the sail. He used the salvageable pieces of his broken boat and the scraps floating past, and slowly, piece by piece, his boat was mended. Remade. Reconstructed from the old as well as from the new.

It did not look like it once did, but it would keep afloat. It was enough to catch the wind again, to ride the wave once more.

The boy did not know which direction was home. He did not know if he could ever find home again. But as he turned to look around him, a gust of wind blew into the sail and the boy breathed it deep into his lungs. There was something in the wind that smelled of hope. He let it fill him, placed his hand on the tiller and set sail.

Woven

On the days when I think I have a fighting chance at redemption, at change, I understand it to be these words and these rituals and these people who will change me. Some days I am not sure if my faith is riddled with doubt or whether, graciously, my doubt is riddled with faith. And yet I continue to live in the world the way a religious person lives in the world; I keep living in a world that I know to be enchanted, and not left alone. I doubt; I am uncertain; I am restless, prone to wander. And yet glimmers of holy keep interrupting my gaze.

Lauren Winner[60]

Being saved, again

The car was full. Not with people but with stuff. Lots of it. Boxes stacked to the roof. Bags and clothes and suitcases and paintings and books and food.

It was a small car and right now it was overflowing. A cardboard box balanced precariously on my right shoulder. My left arm pressed back into a wall of knick-knacks trying to stop it falling onto the gear stick. My head was pushed at an awkward angle by the threatening avalanche behind me. I had bags on either side of my legs and desperately hoped nothing would fall beneath the brakes. This was not a safe way to drive, but there was no other choice.

To make matters worse, the rain pelted down. A flood of water outside to join the avalanche inside. The windscreen wipers chased each other. The water ignored them. I strained to see through the torrent.

Another passenger was squashed into the car with me. Christie. She did not seem to notice the pouring rain on the window. Her head was in her hands. She sat crying in the passenger seat, her body shaking, black mascara a stain down her cheek. Her face was half hidden behind two full bags and a small wooden music box – the sacred items that sat heavy in her lap.

What we carried stacked high in my car were all the possessions she owned. She and her partner. She tried to hold back a whimper but the strangled cat of its grief broke free. A sob pierced the air, louder than the rain. It had been one hell of a day. It had been one hell of a life. My life and its issues were a beachside vacation in comparison.

My wife and I had been living in Melbourne for a few years at this point. I had finished up as the youth pastor of the church I had grown up in and we had moved ten hours south for me to study at a theology college. This was the place that had begun to give me language to articulate what I was trying to believe in – new words that had not been in the cultural lexicon of my old evangelical church fishbowl. I had felt more and more on the outer of my nurturing community until we had finally left and travelled south.

In the beginning of our life in Melbourne, my wife and I were 'between churches'. This is Christian-speak for not going to church but feeling like we probably should. At some point we started going to a house church because we couldn't stomach being at a 'normal' church any longer. Actually, my wife had not been able to stomach being at a 'normal' church for some years now, but I wanted to persist. I wanted to try being at a 'normal' church after our move to Melbourne. After only a few months, though, we began to hit much of the same culture that had given me a rash at my old church. So we moved from mainstream church to 'between churches' to finally settling in a house church.

The house church was really just a handful of other young adults who also couldn't handle 'normal' church at that point in their lives. We would meet around a meal and chat and pray, and someone would bring something theological to talk through.

We knew what we didn't want our Christianity to look like and this was our fledgling attempt at trying to work out what it might. This was our endeavour to hold it together still, only now outside the confines of mainstream church. This was us trying not to simply throw in the towel but to continue walking through the desert of unravelling. There was little pretence in the house church, and there was realness and open conversation. Without my realising it, these things were working a slow healing inside.

Around the same time, I started helping out at a local soup kitchen, trying to match my rhetoric with my reality. I had been waking up to the broken hierarchy of our world for some time now. Unravelling and raging and wrestling and doubting. It was a constant deconstruction. But by then, to be honest, I was getting sick of my own cynicism.

I needed something I could actively give myself to.

One night I went down to the basement of a local church building where I heard they gave dinner to people who needed a meal. I helped out with the serving and then sat around talking. This is when I met Christie. It was six months later that she sat in the passenger seat with her head in her hands and the tears falling.

Christie and her partner, Andrew, were both heroin addicts. Addicts who, like many, were trying as hard as they could to get clean. Both were on the methadone program, desperately fighting their addiction.

Christie talked more than most and certainly faster than anyone else I had ever met. This, coupled with the nervous twitches, slight shaking and obvious agitation throughout her body caused by years of addiction, made her words come out tumbled. Washing-machine words. Turned in circles in her mouth and confused.

To understand her you had to put the pieces of her thoughts together in the right way. It was a puzzle. When you solved the puzzle, what you heard was a caring thought towards her partner, or a cry of desperation, or a declaration of determination, or a theory on God and the universe, or some profound and beautiful insight into life and love and loss. A deep wisdom was hidden beneath the shaking body of her addiction and the puzzle pieces of her words.

One week, Christie told me the story of her life. Broken family. Broken bones. Broken promises. Broken home. A life of desperation and struggle and drugs and hunger and dreams and hope. Always the hope. Always the fight. Her life was the very opposite of my own sheltered upbringing, my mansion on the hill.

This was why I had gone to the soup kitchen in the first place. I wanted to live out a new way of being in the world. But I still carried with me all of my old evangelical zeal for wanting to save people and put on my chest the badge for doing so. I thought these people needed my help. I thought I had it together and they did not. Such is the ignorance of the saviour complex. The colonialist missionary kid of my teens was still in there, still governing how I saw the world.

It takes someone like Christie to shatter one's ignorance and show blindness for what it is. Each week, for several months, I took her and Andrew to the chemist to get their methadone. As we went, I could see the way others avoided them – how people looked with judgement as these friends of mine bent to pick up half-used cigarette butts from the gutters. I ate meals with them and we talked and laughed and cried and dreamed of better days. They told me, through gritted teeth, of their financial difficulties but refused to take money to help out. They said they were the ones who had got themselves into their mess so they needed to get themselves out of it. This was a hard one for me to take – me, who had so much I could give them; me, who wanted to save them.

I remember the day Christie broke down in tears because she had promised Andrew she would no longer steal from the shops and yet that morning had given in and stolen a packet of coffee. She was racked with guilt at having broken her word to him. She desperately wanted to be a better person.

Everything about these two was a determined fight for a better life. A fight against the drugs that broke them and tore them apart from each other. The poison they injected, the slow death. Yet, in the time I spent with them, I was with some of the most generous, kind-hearted, authentic, forgiving and encouraging people I have ever met. They taught me; I did not teach them. They were saving me: saving me from my ignorance, from my ego, from my need to save them. Saving me from myself.

Jesus always comes to us disguised.

It makes me think of the Dead Marshes scene in *The Lord of the Rings*. Frodo cannot take the Ring to Mordor by himself; he needs Samwise beside him. But even then, they cannot do it alone. So who takes them through the Dead Marshes? Who guides their path and shows them the way forward?

It is Gollum. The addict who is Gollum. They need him. He saves them. He gets them through the marshes.

Jesus on the earth

I received the call late one night. A hysterical Christie was on the other end of the phone. Her words were even more disjointed than usual. 'Throwing rocks ... kicked out ... drugs ... baseball bat' – this was all I could make out. My heart beat faster. I could hear her fear.

She passed the phone to Andrew and things became a little clearer.

They had been living in a small cottage out the front of their dealer's house. I had been to their little home a few times, but they had never told me who the owner was. They had fallen behind in their 'unofficial' rent because the week before they had relapsed and used again. This led to a large argument with the landlord-dealer, who had turned off their electricity and started throwing rocks at them if they came outside the little hut. He gave them till the next morning to be out or his friends would physically throw them out. Now he was standing on his front verandah with a baseball bat at his side.

This is when Christie rang me. Scared white and panicking. Shaking even more than usual.

I drove to their home, also scared white and shaking more than usual. Thankfully their dealer had gone back inside by the time I arrived. Their little lounge room was candle lit and full of fear. They had started putting all they owned into whatever boxes or bags they could find. These were then hurriedly jammed into every corner of my car.

We packed as fast as we could go. About an hour later, Andrew left on his pushbike to meet us later at Christie's mum's. I stood beside Christie as she packed the last of her stuff. She stopped for a moment and stared down at a locket in her hand. She looked up at me and said she was proud of herself. I told her I was proud of her too, and I asked her what made her say so. She told me it was because she had managed to keep so many things that were precious to her.

'No other junkies I know can say that for themselves,' she told me, piling old diaries into her bag.

The very last thing on the coffee table, next to the dripping wax candle, was her music box. I opened it and listened to the tinkle and stared at the little dancing girl twirling around in the candlelight. *I* felt like this dancing girl, trapped inside my own music box. The comfort and ignorance and tinkle of a seductive tune. I had been so blind to the harshness and raw inhumanity of the world, to what my friend Christie had to face every day.

An hour later, through storm and stress and holding back the avalanche in my car, we arrived at her mother's house. The car was unloaded. We were soaked through. Half an hour later we were wrapped in towels and sipping a cup of tea together, trying to get warm and dry again.

As she sipped her tea, Christie suddenly coughed as she swallowed, looked up at me and blurted out, 'I believe in Jesus.'

'Yeah?' I said, somewhat taken back by this statement out of the middle of nowhere. 'You know, I do too.' And I found myself, for the first time in a long while, really meaning it. Believing it.

She went on to tell me that Jesus was a healer, and that he would connect with people, and listen, and bring them love and peace, and do whatever he could for them. This is the Jesus she believed in. I agreed. She then looked at me – really looked at me. She held the moment between us, her face still ashen with the shock of the day, her skin pockmarked and tight, her eyes jittery, her hands shaking. She placed one of these shaking hands on my own.

'Joel,' she said slowly, focusing intently on the depth of meaning in her words, not wanting them to come out jumbled. 'You do this, too. You do whatever you can. You love. You heal. Joel, you are my Jesus. You are Jesus on the earth today. You are Jesus to me.'

It was the greatest compliment I have ever received. Not that it was my compliment. Or not a compliment I could just receive without recognising that it was actually a compliment directed above me. To the

Jesus she was seeing in me. The Jesus in me. She helped me to see him once again. I had come to save her and she saved me. She saved my faith. She restored my belief in Jesus and made me realise I was following him still, even if following him wasn't what I thought it would be.

A few minutes later I was back in the now empty car. It had never felt so cavernous before. I drove down the street but had to pull over to the curb. I could not see through my tears. I sat there sobbing. The emotional intensity of the day finally caught up with me and I broke.

But this breaking wasn't like the breaking that had been over the previous few years. This was not a further unravelling. Somehow, in this breaking, I was actually being put back together again.

God still did not make sense, the Bible was still a blur, Christianity was still flawed, the church was still full of hypocrisy and politics – yet as I sat there crying, my tears felt as though they were nothing but worship.

A thread of hope began to find a weave inside me. Hope. It is the first movement into the Woven. It begins as a ripple and then, overtime, can become a flood. This is how it was for me.

Weaving the threads

It is a few years on now as I write these words about Christie. I sit beside a fireplace with my wife. I look up from the flames to see her in the throes of her first-time knitting project. A blanket. It will soon become the baby blanket for our first child. A knitted warmth. A blanket held together not by glue or staples or any form of external fixing, but by tension. An intricate and detailed pattern of tension.

One knit. One pearl. One knit. One pearl. One strand wrapped around another, around another, around another. Each thread pulls the other and, by the opposite force, they each are held in suspension. The threads are woven again and again until a beautiful blanket, an aesthetic pattern of pull and strain, materialises.

The art of weaving, too, upholds a form of design that requires no externals once the tapestry is made. It is held from within. The weaver sits at a loom and interlaces wool with wool. Over and under and over

140

and under. The warp, the vertical thread, and the weft, the horizontal thread, are framed by the loom and so meet each other in a repetition of interwoven beauty.

When you watch an experienced weaver working a loom, it is a captivating sight. A graceful movement. To and fro. My wife's knitting skills do not yet hold such grace; she swears and stares intently at her blanket, trying to work out where she went wrong, which stitch she dropped. I am glad I am a writer and not a knitter, but I too know the many stitches that have been dropped over the years of my unravelling.

Yet still, even in the clumsy first attempts of my wife's needles, there is a rhythm that brings forth beauty. Just like weaving. A woven tapestry is held together in strength and fragility between the embracing frame of the loom. The surrounding structure holds all the pieces. Just as we need a surrounding structure to hold together the threads of our lives. We need a larger story to hold us. That by which the fibre of our existence, the frayed ends of an Unravelled Self, may find their weave, one around the other. We need a loom.

The English word 'text' is derived from *texere*, the Latin word for weaving. What a beautiful etymological connection. A text is a weaving – the weaving of a story, the bringing together of the threads of life into an interwoven, textual whole. Allowing the warp of one story to loop around the weft of another and so to hold each other in tension.

Within the tapestry of the individual, the warp of a story of neglect is held by the weft of a story of love. The warp of the story of the victim is held by the weft of the story of the courageous. The warp of the broken and the weft of the growing. The warp of the light and the weft of the shadow. Within our life each thread is guided by a tender hand, a kind gaze, a reimagining. Each string is held in tension with, supported and embraced by a hundred others.

The Woven Self comes to be when the thread of our life experience and the thread of our spirituality is intentionally woven around the loom of a larger story. That is, when every part of who we are is threaded in with that which is beyond ourselves. When the fibres of our emotionality, our sexuality, our actions, our beliefs, our friendships, our self-perspective, our politics, our physicality, our story are all woven in with this this larger story. In and through, over and under, the Woven Self threads the strands together into something of a blanket – a holistic life, an integrated faith, an intentional mutuality. We are woven in with ourselves and woven in with those around us and woven in with the rest of the world. We are no longer just individual. This is what the larger story calls us to.

The Woven Self is holistic. It is the holding together of the disparate parts of our lives.

The everyday things are woven in and through the sacred things. Over and under.

Our inside world of convictions, beliefs and values is woven in with our outside world of lifestyle, choice and actions. Over and under.

The Other is woven in with the Self. Over and under.

Our body is woven in with our emotions and our thoughts and our deepest core. Over and under.

The material world we walk in is woven in with the spiritual world we walk through. Over and under.

How we shop is woven in with how the rest of the world lives. Over and under.

The personal is woven with the political. Over and under.

Our light and bravery are threaded with our shadow and our frailty. Over and under.

We can sit in the tension of the old answers threading together with new explorations. Over and under.

We can hold together the truths of the sculpted with the doubts of the unravelled. Over and under.

The Woven Self is the realisation that everything, everywhere is connected. That you have been woven into the great pattern of the world, where each individual thread is essential to the weaving of the whole. The many come together to form the one. Every thread is crucial, for every story is crucial.

To live out of the Woven Self is to live in an aesthetic tension that brings together all the threads of life into a holistic tapestry – including those things that do not make sense. And including those things without answers. The Woven do not need to have the answer, they do not need to solve the problem, they do not rage against what has been. They continue the search and find home within the searching.

If the pieces left by the shattering of what was are not thrown away, they may actually become mosaic and beautiful. The too-small clothes, if not tossed out, may become the very patchwork pieces needed to weave the new. A faith rearranged.

The Sculpted Self insists it knows the answer. The Unravelled Self insists that answer is wrong while still wishing there was an answer. The Woven Self offers a third way. An in-between way. The Woven Self is able to sit in the complexity of there not being an easy answer. It honours the mystery of paradox.

The Woven consistently sit in a suspension between opposites such as these.

The spider web is one of nature's most beautiful forms of weaving. It is both aesthetic and functional. It is a place of growth and death and beauty. It is both delicate and incredibly strong. It takes on the buffeting wind and remains connected, retains the beauty of its shape. Strung between two walls, the web is held in place by the tension of where it intersects with the world around. A home in the air.

This Woven spider home is analogous. It upholds a place of home not standing on the solid ground of absolute answers and absolute authority. Rather, the web, like faith, is made strong by holding together the tensions, a weaving of truths and stories, of old answers with new explorations.

The Woven Self embraces the seeming contradictions of life. It sits in the tension of the Scriptures that affirm God's love as eternal and the reality of life that seems to affirm the opposite. The hope we feel, the suffering we see. The intention and the failed action. The Woven Self holds these together, forces them together as a dialogue. And a blanket is woven, and a home is built, and the tension is held and beauty comes from this suspension between the opposites, from this third way. The way of the Woven.

The differences between the three

The *Sculpted Self*, without even realising, does what it does, believes what it believes, because it has been patterned to do so. It has been conditioned by a script, a set of rules. A fishbowl.

The *Unravelled Self* begins to name this reality. It realises its path has been shaped by others. It no longer denies these social scripts but names them and rejects many of them, often thinking it can do better its own way.

The *Woven Self* knows there is no such 'own way'. It knows it will always be shaped. But it also knows it does not have to be wholly defined by such shaping. Shaped but not dictated. The water will colour our every choice, yes, but it does not have to dominate.

~

The Sculpted Self is a fenced and bounded existence. It is stringent edges and high walls, a circumference that is solid and sure. It is the upholding of who is in and who is out based on correct belief and correct behaviour. It is the delineation of right and wrong, good and bad, orthodox and heretical. There is a safety inside fences where the sheep can go no further than the border.

The Unravelled Self is a breaking down of these fences. It is smashing down the walls to live in the freedom of being fenceless. It is wandering out into the wilderness. Sadly, it too easily leads to starvation as the sheep are seldom guided by others to find food and water along the way. The Unravelled cannot handle the fenceless life for too long as it has no central watering hole to come back to.

The Woven Self no longer needs the fences, yet it realises that true freedom comes not from simply being fenceless. True freedom means staying close to the watering hole so that one does not die of thirst. It is living out of the inner wellspring that sits at the centre of one's life. The Woven may never again look like those inside the fence. They do not need the fences of external rules because now they drink from the watering hole of their deep convictions. This water flows into the values

144

by which they live their lives, and these values flow into their actions and their practices.

~

The Sculpted Self has a socialised faith. The Unravelled Self has a searching faith. The Woven Self owns the faith it has come to and acknowledges both the socialised and the searching within it.

The Sculpted Self is shaped by the external rules, the expectations, the authority of the community. The Unravelled Self is shaped by a breaking out from these external rules and expectations. The Woven Self chooses to live out of its own internal, intrinsic values.

The Sculpted Self upholds the notion (implicitly and explicitly) that you must believe the right things and behave the right way and then you can belong. The Unravelled Self challenges the beliefs, bends and breaks the behavioural rules and says, 'I don't need to belong.' The Woven Self says, 'You *belong*, first and foremost, and always; no matter what, you belong. And then, in your belonging, you may find that your behaving and believing go through their own becoming.'

The Sculpted Self focuses on construction. The Unravelled Self focuses on deconstruction. The Woven Self focuses on reconstruction – that is, on the bringing together of a far more flexible and meaningful system that is able to hold in its frame the increasing complexities of life.

The Sculpted Self is blind to hypocrisy. The Unravelled Self demands that the Sculpted Self admit its hypocrisy. The Woven Self knows it suffers the same hypocrisy. Such a knowing allows grace to sit in the midst of the hypocrisy and learning and growth to take place in this space. It does not hold back when hypocrisy must be challenged, yet it also does not have to rage in rebellion against it.

The Sculpted Self has a defensive posture, the Unravelled Self an offensive one. The Woven Self seeks to hold open hands towards what comes.

The Sculpted Self is focused on solid structure. The Unravelled Self is the breaking of this structure. The Woven Self is about knowing those things to adopt and reinterpret and reintegrate from the structure that was, and what things to leave behind.

The Sculpted Self holds too tightly. The Unravelled Self throws out too quickly. The Woven Self learns how to hold loosely, yet close to the heart.

The Sculpted Self fights to prove the authority of its fishbowl. The Unravelled Self fights to escape the fishbowl. The Woven Self knows that the journey out of one fishbowl inevitably leads you into another.

The Sculpted Self yells the answers. The Unravelled Self yells back. The Woven Self stops shouting and tries to start listening.

The Sculpted Self knows it is right. The Unravelled Self knows the Sculpted Self is wrong. The Woven Self knows there is always more happening than right and wrong.

The Sculpted Self has everything ordered and secure. The chaos of the Unravelled Self finds no place to lay down and rest. The Woven Self knows both the dangers of what is ordered and the dangers of being tossed by the chaos. It chooses to anchor itself in the midst of both.

The Sculpted Self ignores the contradictions. The Unravelled Self points out the contradictions. The Woven Self takes into itself the contradictions and allows the soul to settle into the tension of them. It is an amalgamation.

The Sculpted Self is all about what you know. The Unravelled Self is all about questioning what you thought you knew. The Woven Self is knowing that you do not know, and being OK with this so as to learn from different perspectives.

The Sculpted Self is dependent. The Unravelled Self is independent. The Woven Self is radically interdependent.

The Sculpted Self seeks to convert others to its way of thinking. The Unravelled Self seeks to convert others to its questioning. The Woven Self allows people to convert themselves, holding up the truth that it is OK for you to believe differently. It says, 'I do not need to fight you. I do not need to argue with you. We can sit and learn from each other, and I can hold your truth in tension with my own.'

The Sculpted Self is thesis, the Unravelled Self is antithesis, but the Woven Self is synthesis. It sits in the third way. It holds thesis and antithesis together, recognising that both sides of an argument need each other. They can exist side-by-side together. Their liberation is caught up with the other.

The Woven Self knows that life can be full of pain and this pain can be full of joy. It knows that God can be as close as the skin and at the same time far away. It understands that to find life you must lose life. It realises that the poor are blessed and the rich are actually poor. The Woven Self does not run from paradoxical tensions, but rather embraces the learnings to be found within them.

~

Of course, it must be reiterated here that in real life things are never so neat and tidy. There are always parts of me sculpted, parts unravelling and parts finding a weave. All the time.

But the overall movement is clear. It is from a socialised, conformist, inherited, uncritical faith, the product of being raised in a particular nurturing community, through a searching, questioning, doubting, critiquing, accusing unravelling, to slowly find oneself in some form of owned, internalised, integrated, holistic way of being in the world.

This way of being may look very different from who you once were, but it has become the place you now call home.

A Woven Home

Look, I find the clergymen's God as dead as a doornail. But does that make me an atheist? The clergymen think me one – be that as it may – but look, I love, and how could I feel love if I myself weren't alive and others weren't alive? And if we live, there's something wondrous about it. Call it God or human nature or what you will, but there's a certain something that I can't define in a system, even though it's very much alive and real, and you see, for me it's God or just as good as God ... to believe in God, by that I mean feeling that there is a God, not a dead or stuffed God, but a living one who pushes us with irresistible force in the direction of 'Love on'. That's what I think.

Vincent van Gogh[61]

Nomadic dwelling

The fireplace by whose light I write now is in the lounge room of the 500-year-old house where we are staying on the Holy Island of Lindisfarne. This is where my wife has taken up her new hobby of knitting. We sit by the fireplace and she clicks needles together and I write out the stories. We both drink whisky. There is not a lot to do on a frozen island in the middle of winter.

We have been here a few months now and are soon to return to Australia. Sitting by the fireplace has become a favourite pastime. It is certainly one I can live with. A fireplace, a hearth – the heart of the home – holds a special sacredness and a deep presence. The whisky helps too.

We watch the flicker and I listen to the constant tick, tick of the needles as I think back to what has brought us to this place. To who I am now. I think back over the last few years and realise that what was once so disjointed and fractured, what was so many threads unravelled, has slowly come together to find a new weave inside this life I call my own.

It feels as though I have found my way home. Not to the old home;

I am not at the doorstep of my parents' or my old church's faith and understanding. The reality of my spirituality now looks far different to what it was once sculpted to be. Different, but somehow the same. The same, but somehow different. A translation of faith and belief into the intricacy of who I am: this is what sits at the heart of the Woven.

No, I did not go back home. I found a new home.

Or perhaps it was that a new home somehow found me.

Or perhaps what has actually occurred is that during my wandering a home slowly grew on my back without my even realising. A snail shell to shelter my fragile being. A moving dwelling place. A home that was found in the walking, not in the arriving. Never do we fully arrive – like the Unravelled Self, the Woven Self is a pilgrim. But something had arrived in me.

What had arrived was a knowing that I was home. A knowing that even in the midst of the wilderness, I could find a dwelling place. As tenuous as everything else might be, I could be in the midst of it all and still be OK. I could be at home in whatever circumstance and season. A snail shell. A woven home.

The Woven is not the season of perfect weather, though many think it must be. It is not about perfection outside or inside. Rather, it is to know *home* regardless of winter cold or summer heat, regardless of the shedding of leaves or the beginning of spring. It is to not have to fight against, but to sit within. It is to not have to have it all together, but to know that we will never have it together and that this is OK. The Woven Self is coming home to both the depth and the mess of who one truly is. It is no longer running from something but running towards something. It is being called from ahead, not pushed from behind.

And what was calling me? What was I running towards? What is this home I had found? What had begun a reconstruction, a new weave within and without?

Well, aside from Christie, let me tell you where this new thing began.

A tradition to belong to

It was a Sunday a few years earlier, a while after helping my friends flee from their drug dealer. I was walking by the river in a town called Warrandyte. At that time I knew my old world had gone. I knew that during my passionate early teenage years the evangelical Christian tradition had been my place of belonging; and yet, as time wore on and the unravelling had come, so too had come the sense of lostness, of being on the outer of the culture and community I had grown up in.

I knew the leaving of home. The circle of my own spiritual understandings no longer seemed to fit the triangle hole that had birthed them. I needed something less angled and acute. So I left what was and wandered, and I wandered not knowing really what I was looking for.

For a long time there was just the distaste and the wandering. But by now, walking along that river, I had also begun to realise there were things I could hold on to. Things I *wanted* to hold on to. Things I was coming to own as my own. The unravelled wandering had been sifting me down to the core – getting rid of the cultural dross and the religious paraphernalia. If the unravelling was a dropping of everything, I was once again beginning to hold things in my head and my hands and my heart.

What I held were new learnings and new feelings. New ideas about God. New community. New friends. New understandings. A growing sense of connection with the earth around me. The continued call to justice. The new call to knowing my ancestry. The awakening to parts of myself long dormant: creative parts, hopeful parts, sacred parts. It was the mystery – I was beginning to embrace it. And to not fear that everything was messy.

What I was holding was Jesus. What I was holding was Love and grace and hope. There were still many aspects of my old Christianity that I found myself holding, and there was much that was new.

But with all these things I held, I still didn't know where all the new parts fitted. And in the wider scheme of everything, I still didn't know where *I* fitted. I didn't know if who I now was and what I felt and what I held could belong anywhere. I didn't know if there were a people I could call 'my people', if there was a tradition I could belong to.

I was now beginning to hold again, but I didn't know what or who could hold me in the process. Turns out, it was an Irishman.

~

Beside the river, by the main road, was one of those second-hand bookstores filled with stacked books threatening to tumble. A ramshackle building that was probably once someone's home. The fireplace still remained in the main room, the mantle covered with books. You had to squeeze through shelves trying not to knock any to the ground.

On this day, as I walked past outside, I felt an intuitive whisper that I should go into the shop. I had been learning to listen to these intuitive whispers since my teenage years. Sometimes I got them right, sometimes very wrong. This day I somehow knew there was an orange book in the shop waiting for me. I knew it was in the back room. I knew it was on a bottom shelf.

I do not know how I knew these things. Some would say God told me. Some would say the prophetic. Some would say intuition. Some would say I was losing my mind.

The bell above me jingled as I walked through the door. The lady at the counter looked up and smiled. I went through the front room without stopping all the way to the back. I looked down to my right in that back room and there, in this little bookstore by the river, was the book with the orange cover. I had known it would be there.

What I didn't know was that for the next three years I would carry that book around with me everywhere I went. What I didn't know was that it would be my dearest companion, tattered and scribbled and read and re-read. I picked it up that day, immediately bought it and went and read it by the river.

I read most of it that afternoon. I couldn't put it down. It was telling me who I was.

The book was called *Eternal Echoes: Celtic Reflections on Our Yearning to Belong* by a man named John O'Donohue.[62] I had never heard of him. He was a Celtic, Catholic philosopher, poet and mystic, and that afternoon he changed my life. He was a stranger who gave me a place to belong. Or better to say, he named the place I already belonged but had not known. He was a stranger who told me I wasn't strange; a stranger who introduced me to what would become my home.

John O'Donohue has had more impact on my life than any other writer. I devoured that first book. I bought anything else he had ever written. I listened to his audio books and his interviews. I soaked myself in the thoughts of this mystic, and somewhere in the midst of those pages, in the lilt of his Irish accent, in his reflections on Celtic Christian spirituality, I found myself. It is the only way to explain it. I found where I belonged.

O'Donohue expressed with profundity and eloquence so much of what I had come to believe but had never had the words to express. He named and validated these things I was holding in my hands. In his explorations into the Celtic and contemplative traditions, I found myself. In his reflections on our connection with creation and with the world that sits beneath it all, I found myself. In his delving into the wisdom of the earth and the elements and a God far larger than I ever thought possible, I found myself. In his thoughts on living by a rhythm of life and allowing the outer world to shape the inner world, I found myself. In all these things, he was articulating what I longed for, what I had glimpsed only briefly.

I found myself, for I found my tradition. A tradition that could hold me. A tradition that did not demand my adherence but rather invited me to name what was already taking shape within me. A tradition through which, once again, I could call God home.

It was a greater thread that I could find a weave within.

Tradition is often spoken of with distaste in contemporary society. It is that which locks us in to an old mindset. It is the opposite of freedom. It is dry, dogmatic, mechanical, stodgy. These are exactly the feelings of the Unravelled Self towards tradition.

On the other side of the unravelling, however, there is a reclaiming of tradition. In fact, much of the movement into the Woven is a reclaiming and a renaming of those things that our sculpted reality made too small. It is a redefining of words that were perhaps thrown out during the unravelling: words like grace, worship, sin, born again, evangelism, discipleship, faith, healing, Spirit, hell, heaven, evil, lost, found, prayer, redemption, Christian. Words like tradition. These are all words trying to get at something important if we have the courage to reclaim their intention – to strip them of their baggage and rethink what the truth is they are seeking to name.

To embrace a tradition does not mean that one is traditional, outdated, jammed into a dogmatic obedience. My finding of a tradition was the very opposite. It opened my world and deepened my world. It brought more freedom than I knew possible. It led to exploration and imagination and liberation. It gave me a wider spirituality I could call my own, and a wider community existing across time and space. A framework to hang my life on.

My reconstruction had begun.

I cried often that afternoon by the river as I read the words of this stranger. The intensity of knowing I had been found was overwhelming. Tears of recognition were shed. A man I had never met and never would meet had shown me where I belonged. I cannot overstate the impact. I wasn't just a loner, a wayward heretic on a journey anymore; I was surrounded by those who have gone before me. A rich heritage stretching back through the generations. Back to Saint Patrick. Back to Saint Columba. Back to Saint Brigid. Back to Saint Aidan. I read about these Celtic saints and the lives they lived and the myths they embodied.

I went on and read more and more books about Celtic spirituality. I went on and read my family history. It all explained so much.

Going on pilgrimage

So I also needed to see it. I needed to go there – to the land of my ancestors. To the land of John O'Donohue, who had passed away about the same time I had picked up his orange book that day by the river.

My wife and I left Australia and travelled the world, heading in the direction of Ireland and Scotland. We began in the United States, and within the first few weeks of being there we were at a festival in North Carolina: the Wild Goose Festival. The wild goose is a Celtic symbol for the Holy Spirit. Untamed. Uncontrolled. Unexpected. One who brings disruption. It was somehow appropriate.

I was eating lunch at the festival when a grey-haired man sat beside me to eat his meal. We exchanged pleasantries. He mumbled in a thick Scottish accent, so I leaned in to make out his words. His name was Colin Fraser Wishart. At some point in the conversation I mentioned John O'Donohue. I spoke of how much John's writings had changed my life.

Colin stopped eating and looked up at me, a tear in his eye.

'Oh John,' he said with all the sentiment in the world, 'John was my dear friend.'

Needless to say, the conversation and the friendship grew from there. We were two strangers brought together around our common love for this man who had died only a few years before.

Months later, my wife and I travelled the coast of Ireland and came to John's gravesite. I kneeled at his garden grave, and, as mist flowed down the Irish countryside all around, I read his poetry, and I wrote my own poetry, and I thanked him. I wept the tears of someone who had come to know who he was by the writings of a stranger who was a stranger no longer. A friend whom I had never met.

From Ireland we travelled to Ayrshire in Scotland, to the land of my ancestors. The first McKerrow registered there in 1530. We sailed by ferry from Ireland, and when I saw the coast of Ayrshire, where my people had lived for generations, something completely overwhelmed me. I broke down on the boat. I wept. It was as though I was being welcomed home to a place I had never known. As though the land remembered me. I cannot describe this feeling, but I have spoken to others who have also known it when they were on their own pilgrimages. The landscape around us is always alive and full of presence – so holds the Celtic view of the world.

From Ayrshire we went and stayed with our dear friend from the Wild Goose Festival, Colin Fraser Wishart. He lives in a house by the sea in a town just south of St Andrews and is a man whose own contemplative lifestyle beautifully reflects the heartbeat of his old friend, John O'Donohue. One night while we were there, Colin brought out old home movies of the two of them on a pilgrimage around Ireland, and we talked into the night of what John was like when the world wasn't watching, of who the man was behind those words I had read so many times.

When we left his house to continue our journey, Colin wrapped me in his arms and looked at me with a deep fondness.

'Joel, I want you to know something.' His words held a seriousness that slowed time. 'I want you to know that if John were still alive today, he would really love you.'

Words cannot convey all that this meant. I will not even try.

From Colin's house we came, across the Pilgrim's Way, to this island where we have been living for the last two months. Here we sit in the house owned by the Community of Aidan and Hilda, a contemporary Celtic community founded by Ray Simpson, an elder of the modern form of the tradition. We have talked much with him since our arrival. Three times a day we stop what we are doing and pile into the basement for prayers. I have read book after book from their Celtic library. I write out this story of coming home as my wife knits beside me.

This is the story of how we ended up by this fireplace on such an island. But more, it is the story of my being woven back together – the story of reconstruction. Through it all I have immersed myself in this new way. I have dived into this tradition and its understanding of life and God. In this diving I have found the snail shell of a home carried on my back growing larger and larger to encompass me. There is an expansive place of rest inside this self-knowing.

This is the story of self-knowing. This is the story of being given a language. This is the story of being given a framework to hang my faith upon. The weave of my small story has been threaded into something much larger. My individual self has been threaded in with the world around me, with the sacred around me, with the land around me, with the people around me.

Understanding ourselves in context

Celtic spirituality holds that we are never just a single person Who we are cannot be held within the notion of 'mind, body and spirit' as so many believe. Rather, *mind, body, spirit, land and people* are the threads of our personhood. We cannot understand who we are separate from understanding ourselves in the context of the land we are from, the land where we were born and the land where we now walk. We cannot understand ourselves separate from the people and the stories that came before us – the history that paved the way to our existence. Our ancestors. The great cloud of witnesses.

Our individual selves are so woven in with the world around us that we would be remiss to think of ourselves as just individuals. So many of the great religious traditions and indigenous cultures hold the same. The Woven Self moves away from individual identity to understand the self in the context of others – not in the dependence of the Sculpted but with a sense of self that stems from a place of belonging and interdependence. A spirituality that is integrated.

I grew up between the mountains and the sea, on the east coast of Australia at the base of Mount Keira – or, as the Indigenous peoples of the area call her, 'Geera'. Geera, along with her sisters Mimosa, Wilga, Lilli Pilli, Wattle and Clematis, were the daughters of Oola-boola-woo, the West Wind. According to Indigenous mythology, these children were naughty and as punishment Geera's sisters were thrown into the sea and became the five islands that lie just off the coast of Wollongong. Geera was left alone on top of the escarpment. There she would bend over to watch the lives of the local Aboriginal tribes and look out to sea to see her sisters. Eventually she turned to stone and the dust and leaves and earth built up around her so that she became part of the escarpment.

It is there she now stays. Watching. Waiting. She watched the day I was born below the mountain. She watched me grow from child to man.

This was the landscape that held me as a child and teenager. This was the land of my birth. I was formed and watched over by the land that holds together the mountains and the ocean. The silent peaks and the curved valleys. The constant ebb and flow of the ocean's tides washing up onto the shore.

We would go down to the beach in the summer sun whenever we could, and there we would fling ourselves into the chaos of the waves. We would sit out upon the rolling seas on our boards and watch the sun gather in the day and take it behind the mountains. We would sit out on a jetty with my dad catching fish and learning life. This was my place in the world: the sea salt ingrained in my skin, the wildness of the ocean, the patience of the mountain, the giving of the valleys. This was what gave me my sense of being, my place of home.

We are dependent on this mother as a newborn. It is high time we bring to her the honour she deserves. For the earth is graceful in the way she opens up such a space within herself for us to dwell during our short lifetime. Indeed, as soon as we were birthed into existence, we arrived in a physical reality where *place* opened up a *space* for us to inhabit. How we go about inhabiting this space should be a governing reality in our life. A constant shaping force of desire to live in harmony with her, to cultivate the best out of her and to let her call the best out of us.

My evangelical Christian upbringing never upheld land as an important reality to shape one's existence around. Yet well-known Old Testament scholar and theologian Walter Brueggemann says, 'Land is a central, if not *the* central theme of biblical faith'.[63]

To be woven with the land is thus a crucial movement forward, for the spiritual growth of any human occurs always within a particular place, a locale, a landscape, a home. People can fully grow in all facets of who they are only when they realise this and seek to walk in the reality of their feet being upon the earth. We are part of a sacred geography, and it is central to any form of spiritual growth that we seek to attain.

A woven sense of place is when one allows oneself to step back into the presence and rhythm of the landscape around. To live in harmonious mutuality with her. To listen to the stories she is telling. The aesthetic of the landscape is the memory of a place. The landscape tells a story: the story of Geera, the story of the blood in her soil as the Indigenous people were slaughtered upon her by the colonisers.

To learn the narrative of the land you were birthed in and now dwell in is to learn the narrative of your own story. The two are inseparable. You are one with the earth. You can never be separate from her. You may live within her, but she too lives within you.

~

I purposely do not tell more of Celtic Christianity here. My fear is that in doing so you may think it is your answer – that you may seek to appropriate this tradition to solve your own spiritual and life perplexities. It will not. No tradition is the answer. It has much to offer, absolutely. It was the framework that helped me move from an unravelled existence into a woven way of being. But for others it may be the very sculpted reality they need to break from. Celtic Christianity is a fishbowl like any other tradition.

The point of sharing this journey is to show that just as the unravelling of my life was brought on by a few key inciting events that led to years of travelling in what felt like wilderness, so the weaving back together came through a moment or two of direct encounter with a new way of being and then a slow restitching over time. A frog being boiled. Not realising something was changing until it had changed.

The movement into the Woven often comes silently. Without fanfare. It comes

> through community
> through vulnerable conversations
> through people willing to come alongside the Unravelled
> through books
> through ritual and repetition
> through whispers of intuition
> through pilgrimage
> through questions
> through a 'going through the motions' until the motions become real again
> through dialogue with those who have managed to hold their worlds together

through dialogue with those who have not
through risk
through courage
through persistence.

It came for me one restitch at a time until I am now able to sit here by a fireplace and look inward and see the beautiful tapestry that has been woven together. Slowly woven together without my even realising. Now it is a blanket to keep me warm in the winter – a place of belonging. I call this blanket 'home'. I wrap it around my shoulders.

The weaving came one restitch at a time until today I am still a Christian, and a passionate one at that. But it is a passion that looks very different to what it once did, and it is a Christianity that looks very different to what it once did. I have learned slowly over the years to be OK with this. I hope you are too. In fact, I have learned to not just be OK with it but to cherish it and love it.

Indeed, it was amongst the poetry and pages of John O'Donohue's book that I then began to fall in love again with another book. Another text, one too filled with poetry and story and hope. One breathed on by the Divine. One I had been wrestling with ever since I was a boy. One that I had questioned and critiqued during my unravelling, yet now one I too came back to find a home within. One in whose pages I began to see my small story finding a weave into a much grander narrative.

The sculpting community of my childhood taught me to memorise Bible verses and gave me a love of the sacred Scriptures, but they never taught me that I was a continuation of its story. That when I read the story of Peter or James or John, I was not just reading their individual stories, I was reading the Peter part of *the* story, the James part of *the* story. And that I too was now living out the Joel part of *the* story. That I too was woven into, not just the Celtic tradition, but that in fact I was woven in with the great story of a God who loved God's creation and in this love invited her into some kind of beautiful, holistic connection with Godself and with all that God has made. I realised that *my* small story was a part of *our* story. That I had an '*our*', a tribe, a tradition.

And in that sense of belonging I came to know that *our* story is just a small part of a much larger story, *the* story. A story that is spacious and gracious and generous and inclusive enough to hold all the stories everywhere within its open pages.

This is the ultimate weaving. My small story woven in with a story that could hold everything together, all the pain and the darkness and the sorrow held hand-in-hand with redemption and salvation and the hope of what is to come. A God who descends into the broken world. A God who stays there. In the darkness. Who doesn't lord it over, who doesn't click Divine fingers to make it all better. Rather, a God who takes the very darkness into Godself. The world's darkness. My darkness.

The whole story of Jesus and the incarnation, the cross and the resurrection, began to take a hold of me once more. Not just as way to 'get my butt into heaven', but as the very thread whereby the entire universe is brought back into the weave, into the oneness it was made for.

And so it was here indeed that so many of those old words, those thrown out during the unravelling, began to be reinstated in my life. Just in a new way. A woven way. I did not have to reject it all. I could see them renamed. Redeemed. It was the grace that I desperately needed because of a shadow side that never leaves. Worship as the way I live out my life in the everyday. Sin I came to understand as the line of evil and selfish privilege that runs down the centre of each of us and all our societal systems. And how I need to be birthed once more, born once again, born again into the expansiveness of a totally unconditional love and such a grand story. This story. This is salvation. The reframing of a word that once was tainted. Now whole. Now beautiful. Now so very large and so very loving. These words were finding a new meaning. Some were still 'hard to swallow', but it was happening. This reconstructing. This weaving. This sitting in between the old and the new.

In the pages of the Bible, now seen through a less sculpted lens, now seen through a woven and narrative lens, I fell in love once more with the Jesus that I found in its pages. That is the only way I can describe it. It began with an orange book and a tradition that I could belong to, which led me to a Bible I could now love again and a Jesus I could follow again.

Once more, yet very different to what it once was. Same. Same. But different. One stitch and one stitch. Woven back together. A garment for any season of faith and doubt and wrestle and struggle.

It came one restitch at a time until now I no longer fight against the seasons of my life. The times of absence. The times of joy. The times of plenty. The times of betrayal. The times of silence. The times of chorus. The Woven Self comes to accept the rhythms of the seasons and so to flow with their movement. Caught up in the great story.

A weave that is a blanket, warm enough for a cold winter.

A weave that is a shade cloth, large enough for a hot summer.

A weave that is a kite, light enough to catch the winds of autumn.

A weave that is a picnic rug, wide enough for the beauty of spring.

A Woven Society

This hour in history needs a dedicated circle of transformed nonconformists ... Our planet teeters on the brink of atomic annihilation; dangerous passions of pride, hatred and selfishness are enthroned in our lives; truth lies prostrate on the rugged hills of nameless calvaries; and men do reverence before false gods of nationalism and materialism. The saving of our world from pending doom will come, not through the complacent adjustment of the conforming majority, but through the creative maladjustment of a nonconforming minority.

Martin Luther King Jr[64]

The lament of the poet

I stood at the back of the bar and listened to the lament of the poet. A sorrowful keening. He had been unravelling for a long time, filled with rage at being told he was 'not right', at being misunderstood. A gay young man with conservative Christian parents. Their rejection of him due to his sexuality was a callous knife. They were parents who had done all they could to 'cut the gay out of him'; parents from whom he felt nothing but judgement; parents who were scared and whose fear translated into rejection. A teenage boy had been abandoned in the name of 'Christian morality'. The image of God had been cast aside to uphold their particular doctrine.

His pink hair flared bright in its loud rebellion. The tight denim shorts, shiny bling belt buckle, knee-high boots and sparkling tube top declared that his own path had been chosen. The crack in his voice and the tears in his eyes communicated as much as his words and dress. He raged and wept, and rightly so. I let every bullet of his angry words pierce my skin. Too many times I have heard this story. Too many times.

I stood at the bar and began to rage with him. I felt the rising anger at the tradition I grew up in – my sculpted community which had done so much damage out of fear. The hypocrisy. The narrowness. The destruction of a person to uphold a moral. A Christianity of judgement. All in the name of a Christ who only ever gave love to those who were on the 'outside'. A Christ who only ever raged against the religious, pious in-crowd, the elite who dictated who was in and who was out. A Christ who was absolutely accepting and who looked nothing like this man's parents. A Christ who looked nothing like ... me.

The thought struck me like a fist. *A Christ who looks nothing like ... me.* I whispered it out loud as I stood there. The words slapped the rage right out of me. My rising anger fell to the floor. Within a few seconds I went from storm clouds to something else entirely. In the past I would have been caught up in the rage and the blame and the indignation and the pointing finger. I would have forsworn the church once more. Yet now, something was different.

I stood at the back of the bar and listened to the lament of the poet, and somehow I was able to recognise my own place in it. My lament joined his lament. But also something other came up in me: a growing realisation that I had spent many years pointing my finger at the hypocrisy of my sculpting community and had never once truly owned it for myself. In that moment, the finger pointing outwards began to turn itself inward. Not in judgement and self-condemnation – it was not a harsh self-criticism to drown me in guilt and shame. Rather, it was a deep recognition. A knowing. An awareness that set me free from blunt judgement.

In that moment, it became clear that I am a complex mass of intention and broken promises and selfish actions and arrogant criticism, just as my faith tradition is. I, too, am complicit in the madness. I am part of the system, just as the poet's parents are part of the system. The personal is always larger than the individual. I am more than just me. I am one with those who have gone before me. Even more, I am one with the whole of humanity, both its brokenness and its hoping, its selfishness and its compassion. The good and the bad all flows through me. It was the Russian novelist Aleksandr Solzhenitsyn who said that the line of evil does not run between *us* and *them* but 'cuts through the heart of every human being. And who is willing to destroy a piece of his own heart?'[65]

In that moment, the hypocrisy of the man's parents became my own hypocrisy. And my own hypocrisy became the hypocrisy of the world. Their judgements were my own, and their judgements were ours. The fear that led to their actions is the same fear that saturates my own actions, just as it stains the world with its taint. We are all pink-haired. We are all fearful parents. We are light and we are dark. Sinner and saint.

In that moment, the fractured love of the man's parents became my own fractured love. And my own fractured love became the fractured love of the world.

But that was not all. In the same moment as I was able to admit my complicity, *our* complicity, something surprising happened. Strangely, unbelievably, I found I was able to forgive myself for it, and forgive ourselves for it.

I stood at the back of the bar and listened to the lament of the poet, and I broke. I wept, though not tears of regret. They were, somehow, tears of freedom. A knowing of open-handed recognition and forgiveness. The poet may not be able to forgive his parents, and it is not my place to say he must. But I forgive them as I forgive myself. I forgive *us* as I forgive myself.

It is also not my place to tell *you* not to rage and lament. That may be the very thing you need to do to expel what has been done to you. I will not take this away from you.

I simply tell you my experience in that moment. Something took the bitterness out of the anger; something took the resentment and the acrimony. And I was left with the knowing that I am connected to the poet as I am connected to his parents as I am connected to a broken faith tradition as I am connected to those it has broken. I am connected. We are connected. We are woven. Every accusatory, pointing finger is inevitably pointing at a mirror. Likewise, every act of forgiveness towards another breaks the chains from my own ankles. The doorway from the Unravelled into the Woven is a turning around of the finger that points outward and allowing it to point inward. Not in a harsh cycle of judgement and self-punishment, but in acceptance and recognition and transfiguration.

You may not be able to forgive. They certainly may not deserve it. But I wonder if holding on to all that resentment is doing just as much damage as the initial wounding. I wonder what it would look like to at least forgive yourself. To let yourself off the hook. In doing so we are able to cast from us the hold that such resentment has on us. To forgive ourselves. To be forgiven. A surrender into graciousness.

I wonder if, in the process of this forgiveness, you would in fact be forgiving us all.

~

The day the child realises that all adults are imperfect he becomes an adolescent, the day he forgives them he becomes an adult and the day he forgives himself he becomes wise.

Alden Nowlan[66]

Confession

I had changed. I hadn't realised it until I stood at the back of the bar and anger slipped from my back and was replaced with a humble recognition and the knowing of my place in the wider weave of humanity. I did not have to get defensive as the Sculpted Self would, and I did not have to rage and blame or deny the Christian part of me as the Unravelled Self would. I could hold this space and find myself within it.

I had changed. I stood at the back of the bar and listened to the lament of the poet and noticed that the Unravelled Self was not so prominent in me anymore. A new posture had taken over. What had been shattered within me had been rebuilt. The frayed and untethered ends had found a new weave.

I no longer needed to point the finger. I no longer needed to hold Christianity to ransom.

I walked up to the poet as he stepped from the stage, embraced him and said, 'I am sorry.' It was not just one man saying sorry to another man, or just one Christian man saying sorry to a gay man on behalf of Christianity. Rather, it was humanity saying sorry to humanity on behalf of humanity. He looked me in the eyes and kissed me on the cheek.

The next day I wrote him a poem. Indeed, the next day I wrote a series of poems. They were poems of ownership. Poems of lament. Poems of confession. Poems asking for forgiveness. My writing of them was my forgiving, my letting go. I let the lament find a voice in me and I held it the same way I hold anything precious. Gently. With open hands.

The series of four poems begins with the words

I grew up a white man.
I grew up a rich man.
I grew up a Christian man.
I grew up a man.
And for each and every one of these I need to say, I am sorry.[67]

They were a confession from humanity to humanity – a confession of my privilege.

The poems asked us to come together with open arms. To sit around a new table. To look the other in the eye. They asked us to set each other free: rich and poor; oppressor and the oppressed; gay and straight and queer and man and woman and non-binary. White and black. Christian and Muslim. And then to begin with confession.

Each of the four pieces made their way into the world and sought out those who needed to hear them. But for me the first time I performed them was perhaps the most meaningful.

It was a few weeks after writing the poems and 150 people were gathered at a bar not too far from where the pink-haired poet had raged. I spoke the four pieces throughout the night at the launch of an organisation I was starting, the Centre for Poetics and Justice.

As I finished and stepped from the stage, a woman came up to me. She was a Muslim lady who wore a blue head scarf. Her face wore her tears.

She looked at me and said, 'I want you to know, on behalf of my Muslim brothers and sisters, in whatever way I can, I accept your apology for what has been done by Christians to our kind.'

Tears fell from her eyes. Tears fell from mine.

She continued, 'And I would ask the same of you, for what has been done by my people towards yours, for what atrocities have been done in the name of Allah. Would you forgive us?'

I could have died content in that moment. A life complete. My personal confession had found a communal expression. I was instantly woven with my Islamic sister. In a world that say the two of us should be apart and fearing each other, in a world where violence and bigotry occur all the time in the name of Islam and the name of Christianity, in a world so fearful of 'the other' – in this world, I found a dear sister.

Her name is Alia, and she is one of Australia's great poets. Since this time, we have gone on to run workshops and perform together all over Australia. We have stood side-by-side and spoken time and again of a better way of relating and being in this world. We have stood side-by-side and prayed together before going on stage to perform and share our words.

Culture

My dear friend Alia also taught me to love my own culture. She could have easily seen me and my whiteness and decided not to engage in friendship and in working together. I would not have blamed her. But instead she embraced me. She taught me. Through our many discussions, through our work together, she showed me that just as she had her Eritrean culture, so too, beneath my whiteness, was culture, and it was a culture I could be proud of. Not proud of whiteness as a system, which is a force that blankets everything. That is part of my story, but it is not the entirety.

I am from a people. I am from a family. I am from a heritage. I am from a history. My ancestors were from Ayrshire, Scotland, and their Scottish blood still runs through these veins. This is my story.

While I cannot avoid being a part of this social system of privilege, while I will always be a part of the minority who are endowed by the system with advantage, I have come to learn that I must do what I can to stand against the inherent racism of this system. I must stand against the domination and the entitlement and the oppressive structures. I must denounce the system of colonisation that stole the deep story of who a people were when it took them from their land and their family. And I certainly must denounce the perpetuation of this reality in the social systems of our day.

Through all of this, though, I also must discover the deeper story of who I am and be proud of this. I must learn that I have a people. That I am *from* a people. And that it is not the people who are evil. I must learn that culture matters – my culture. I, too, must be proud of this culture, just as I hope you are proud of yours. I am not proud of its dominance, its privilege, its power, its bigotry, and I am not blind to its frailty. Yet when you peel back the system of whiteness, there is always beneath it a deep richness.

Whiteness paints over distinctiveness. It is time to peel away the white paint, to uncover the diversity of our common humanity. It is rainbow, and oh, so beautiful.

I have said sorry and will continue to say sorry for the rest of my life, but I cannot just stop with sorry. White guilt, Christian guilt, middle-class guilt, heterosexual guilt – it is all the same, all born of shame. And I must move from the shame. So I give my actions and my energy. I give my passion and my poetry. And most of all, I give my friendship. May everything I do honour my history and honour your history. I promise I will try as much as I can to not delegitimise you or your culture by being proud of my own. I promise I will do what I can to not further colonise the way forward.

To live woven in this society, then, is to own that I am *white, male, Christian, rich, able-bodied* and *heterosexual*, and that therefore there is a system biased towards me. It is to challenge this system and its reality. It is to listen well to the stories of those not in my fishbowl. It is to amplify their voices. It is to stand alongside them in the pursuance of justice. It is to uncover the deeper story of my own culture and come to embrace it and be woven in with it. It is to uncover and come to embrace a masculinity that is as healthy and whole as I can be and so be woven in with it. It to embrace a generosity in how I live and what I do with my wealth, and so to live economically woven in with the world.

On the fence

What I found fascinating was that Alia told me her own story of unravelling from her sculpted community and of finding herself again. Of being a teenager and choosing to reclaim the wearing of the hijab, of discovering what her faith looked like on the other side of growing up in a Muslim family. She is a Muslim now because she has chosen to be. Her beliefs have been rewoven with her life. She is one of the most stunning and dignified people I know. I have not tried to convert her to my belief system and she has not tried to convert me to hers. Instead, I have learned more from her about God and life and spirituality than I could put into words. We come from such difference, and we find that which weaves us together.

The reality of animosity in our society is ever present. The fence between us, broken. The push towards separation comes from both sides; walls are held up by both sides. Right versus left. White versus black. Men versus women. Christian versus atheist versus Muslim. Pro-life versus pro-choice. Our voices rise till we cannot hear the cries of those forgotten in the middle of it all. We fight our wars and we forget the people caught up in them.

My friend Helen was one of these. One of the forgotten. She faced a crisis pregnancy at 20 years of age, her boyfriend left and she became a single mum with minimum support from anywhere. All she experienced throughout her pregnancy was the fighting of the pro-lifers and the pro-choicers. Mouths open and arguing, but no one from either side coming to help her.

After experiencing this herself and seeing it time and again in our society, Helen started an organisation called The Babes Project (www.thebabesproject.com.au), which specifically provides care and support for mothers going through some kind of crisis pregnancy. As an organisation they are not politically pro-life and they are not politically pro-choice. They stand in the gap between the two. They stand with those neglected by both sides. They break down the political binary by refusing to put politics above people. Real people. Helen would say that unless you spend time actually supporting those affected, stop sharing your opinion. The world has had enough.

The idiom tells us that it is not good to sit on the fence. Yet Helen makes me wonder if this is exactly where we should be. Between force and retaliation. Between us and them and them and us. Between the violence of our opposing arguments. Between the walls that demarcate. Between two sides there is always a no-man's land where the war-torn gather.

So let us sit on the fence. The Woven Self is a fence-sitter. Not with twiddling thumbs and no opinion, of course – activism has its very needed place. But if we lose sight of the people then we lose sight of the point. Let us sit on the fence, with bandages for the broken, with listening ears to hear their story, with listening ears to hear *our own* story. And let us sit on the fence with chisel in hand, with the hammer and axe of our activism. To swing, to swing, to swing till the wall is torn down. Till *all* the walls are torn down. The Woven Self is a fence-breaker.

Fear and charity

What stops this? What brings out the defensiveness in us when someone names these social realities? What causes us to cross to the other side of the street? What causes us to throw some money at the problems in our world and hope that is enough?

Fear. I would say this force is one of fear.

Between charity and change lies a chasm of indifference. Very few find the courage to cross this chasm. Yet, as with school kids who are too lazy to do their homework, there is usually a deeper force causing our apathy. Fear of change. Fear of the loss of our power. Fear of the uncomfortable.

Our fear widens the gap between charity and true change. Fear calls the gap uncrossable. Fear locks us in place, stationary. Fear always backs the norm. Fear is what causes us to walk past the beggar on the street, or perhaps to give him some money but not ask him his name and so to humanise him. Fear causes us to look the other way when hundreds of innocent children are placed behind bars for seeking safety out of war-torn countries. Fear puts up the high fences. Fear stops us from connecting with those who know different circumstances to our own.

We are afraid that things could get messy and demand from us more than we are willing to give. We are afraid of changing our comfortable lives. I know I am.

Don't get me wrong: charity in and of itself is a beautiful thing. It is one person giving to another. It can save the lives of millions of hungry people and suffering children when a disaster strikes in our world.

Yet it can also be a crippling reality, both for the receiver and the giver. Charity can turn broken people into beggars and those with money into supposed saviours. Charity allows me to give in a way that doesn't cost me but still alleviates my guilt. I can hold the world's problems at arms-length while still feeling I am 'doing my part.'

So while charity is a great first step, it is not enough to bring about the social change needed in our world. To give money to people without addressing the society that stole money from them in the first place is no use at all. As Satish Kumar states, 'The urgent challenge facing the world today is not to give more to the poor, but to take less from the poor.'[68]

This is true justice, moving beyond charity to where our very lifestyle and vocation are changed.

A vocation is a calling – it is what your life is being called to, it is your lifestyle, it is who you are. Fredrick Buechner suggests that vocation is 'To find a niche, an intersection, where the world's deep hunger and your deep gladness meet.'[69] That is, to find a place where the deep suffering and thirst and pain of the world intersects with the stuff that makes you come alive. A place where your passions and who you are and the theology you hold collide headfirst with the social realities around you. This is the place we should be seeking to live in. This is what we should be seeking to shape our lives around. This intersection, this place of calling, is where the threads of our individuality find their weave. It is where the small story of our lives is caught up into the grander story of God's work in the world.

This vocational weaving is what may in fact hold you together and give you that deeper purpose to shape your life around.

This weaving is what may hold your faith together.

This weaving is what may hold the world together.

A woven society and a woven person are interchangeable. One leads to the other. Beyond charity is a vocational weaving. Beyond charity is a compassionate weaving. A compassionate society stems from compassionate people, people willing to go beyond charity when it comes to social realities. People like Father Damien.

~

> Charity depends on the vicissitudes of whim and personal wealth; justice depends on commitment instead of circumstance ... charity provides crumbs from the table ... justice offers a place at the table.
>
> **Bill Moyers**[70]

Father Damien

Hawaii was once a kingdom, from 1810 until its queen was overthrown in 1893. Shortly after this is when American imperialism had its way. In 1865, during the time of the kingdom, the small island of Molokai became the place where those with leprosy were quarantined. Isolated. Abandoned.

Leprosy had been brought to Hawaii by foreign traders and sailors and was thought to be highly contagious (though now we know that 95 percent of humans are immune to the disease). Between 1866 to 1969, around 8000 Hawaiians were sent to the island after contracting the disease.

At the beginning, having little support from the authorities, the leper colonies quickly became the most wretched of places. Molokai was an island of disease and death. The government hoped the leper colony would be able to farm the land and care for itself, but the people were just too sick. They lived in small huts that would be blown over in the wind, leaving the lepers helpless in the face of the elements. They could only lay there in the mud and the blood and wait to die.

A man named Ambrose Hutchinson, a veteran of half a century in the colony, told this story of the place.

A man, his face partly covered below the eyes, with a white rag or handkerchief tied behind his head, was pushing a wheelbarrow loaded with a bundle, which, at first, I mistook for soiled rags. He wheeled it across the yard to a small windowless shack ... The man then half turned over the wheelbarrow and shook it. The bundle (instead of rags it was a human being) rolled out on the floor with an agonizing groan. The fellow turned the wheelbarrow around and wheeled it away, leaving the sick man lying there helpless. After a while the dying man raised and pushed himself in the doorway; he lay there face down.[71]

Life on the island was worse than death. To sit in the decay of one's own body and wait for the soothing touch of death was a miserable existence.

One man, though, came to live on the island who did not have leprosy. He was not sent to the island but chose to go. A Belgian priest named Damien de Veuster. Father Damien went to try and do whatever he could for the people of the colony.

At first he and a few other priests visited for short times to provide food, medical assistance and spiritual accompaniment for those on the island. However, soon Father Damien felt he could no longer just visit the lepers and go back to normal life on the mainland. He did not see why he should have such privilege when those suffering did not. So he eventually set up his home on the island, right there with the lepers, with the full knowledge, according to the medical understanding of the time, that he was certain to contract the disease himself and die from it.

One of his first visits was to a young girl whose whole side he found had been eaten by worms. This kind of horror was an everyday occurrence. Any closed-in room was putrid with the stench of rotting flesh so that Damien had to use tobacco to counteract the odour when he entered. After only six months of being on the island, Damien wrote to his brother, 'I make myself a leper with the lepers.' Indeed, so deep was his solidarity with the abandoned people of Molokai that at one point, although he had not contracted the disease, he began a sermon with the words, 'We lepers ...'

Beyond ignorance, beyond emotional awareness, beyond charity, there lies compassion. First and foremost, compassion is a friend. She is a holding hand. She goes over to the island. She refuses to throw money to people sitting at the bottom of a pit but lowers herself into the pit. Compassion is gentle to some and outraged towards others. She is ferocious. Indignant. She is solidarity. She holds those broken. She is weak for the weak and tears for the crying. She is connection. She is suffering. Her name, Compassion, comes from the Latin words *pati* ('to suffer') and *cum* ('with') and literally means 'to suffer with'.

Compassion sits in the midst of pain without offering clichés and answers. She is the cupped hands catching sweat from the worker in the field. She is the hand holding the hands of the leper. Compassion gives, but not out of her excess. She gives out of that which will cost her.

A woven compassion is the choice to allow the suffering of the world to change who you are. It is a movement towards making poverty personal. It is the weave of one's lifestyle with the reality of an unjust and unequal world. Compassion calls us to go where it hurts and stay there. To immerse ourselves in the sweat and tears and blood and spit of humanity.

At the very centre of the Christian tradition we find a mirror image of Father Damien's life on Molokai in what has been named 'the incarnation'. This is the belief that Jesus was actually the Divine taking on flesh; the Divine taking a step down from divinity and covering himself in humanity. Jesus became a member of an oppressed group of people living under Roman occupation. He walked the dusty streets, sat with the outcasts, cried with the broken, touched the lepers, stood up against the oppressive systems of Roman rule. I have always liked this idea of incarnation, of a God who does not stand above but who puts himself into the midst of a suffering humanity. A God who gives up his power.

When I rage at God for the suffering and hurt and pain and disease I see in the world, when I demand to know why he has not stopped the suffering, I think of Father Damien and of the Christ. And I wonder if God does indeed want to alleviate the suffering of the world but does not want to do it from above. From a position of power. I wonder if he does not want to come in authority and clean away the suffering and the evil, does not want to take away our freedom of choice and the inevitable consequences of this freedom. Rather, I wonder, if God wants to come in love. If God wants to come and take away the suffering by coating divinity in flesh. The flesh of the Christ. The flesh of Father Damien. The flesh of me and the flesh of you.

What if God chooses not to click his fingers and take it all away? What if we are the very vessels through which God is choosing to alleviate the suffering in the world?

Father Damien lived on Molokai for 16 years, working tirelessly to support the sick and dying in whatever way he could. He built homes and furniture for people, ate meals with them, dressed ulcers, dug graves, built a church and a home for the leper's children. He loved them with everyday actions and thoroughly immersed himself in their lives.

Damien urged the lepers of the island to help him in all these activities. He taught them to farm and build and raise animals and play music together. Little by little, the hellish colony changed. As the lepers' dignity was restored, so was their community. They lived now not in miserable isolated shacks that blew over in the wind but in two villages of painted cottages constructed by Damien himself. The cottages were surrounded by flower beds and farmed fields, and in the villages were two orphanages, a hospital and a proper graveyard.

An Englishman named Edward Clifford, who visited the island in 1888, wrote, 'I had gone to Molokai expecting to find it scarcely less dreadful than hell itself ... and the cheerful people, the lovely landscapes, and comparatively painless life were all surprises. These poor people seemed singularly happy.'[72] The island and the lives of these lepers had been radically transformed by this priest. A woven society.

~

It is interesting that the Christ's definition of what was happening through his incarnation into humanity was that 'The kingdom of heaven has come near' (Matthew 4:17). Through this giving of himself to the poor and suffering of the world, he was declaring heaven to be a reality, not up there in the sky somewhere, but right here on the earth, in the midst of an unjust society. Heaven hidden behind a veil until we catch a glimpse of it through acts of justice, mercy, healing, kindness and beauty. Heaven woven in with the earth through acts of compassion.

Jesus called this heaven a 'kingdom'. A kingdom is a king's domain, the rule of a king over a society. Heaven is a new society – a new social order, a new social vision, a new way of being human together. It is not some spiritual plane of existence out there in the ether where we go when we die. We could say that heaven is the reality where God's will happens in perfection, where God's dream for the creation is fulfilled. It is a present reality of individual and societal and spiritual wholeness that will one day splay out into eternity.

Father Damien not only loved the people of Molokai but also stood up for them. He fought for them. He pleaded with the authorities for their wellbeing and care. He went to the government again and again with their cause and was seen by the authorities as 'obstinate, headstrong, brusque and officious'.[73] He knew that to care for his people also meant to stand in solidarity with them. A woven activism.

Compassion, and the new society it may bring about, is more than just befriending and caring for those suffering and adversely affected by the system. Compassion calls for standing against the systems of oppression and standing with those oppressed by them. To care for the sick as they drink water from a poisoned river without ever looking upstream at what is poisoning the river is only ever a short-term solution.

Compassion is a voice challenging the very systems that bring about the suffering. To critique them and to provide an alternative social vision. To suffer with is also to stand in solidarity with. As Dietrich Bonhoeffer wrote in the midst of Nazi Germany, 'We are not to simply bandage the wounds of victims beneath the wheels of injustice, we are to drive a spoke into the wheel itself.'[74]

Compassion calls us to stand up for those who may not be able to stand. Not to speak *for* them but to speak *with* them – to amplify their voice, to link arms around them, to call that which oppresses them to a higher ideal. Compassion calls for a departure from ideologies and activities and vocations that perpetuate inequality in our world. It is a willingness to stand up and challenge the dominant framing story that lies at the heart of the system. It defies and rejects the current ordering of things, no matter the personal cost.

A woven compassion is the weave of one's individuality with the socioeconomic realities one is inevitably part of. It is choosing to care. It is turning away from one's own self-comfort and creating a lifestyle shaped around solidarity. It is choosing not to point fingers but to offer a way forward for all. It is to suffer with, to feel with, to cry and laugh with. To provide an alternative way of being, a new social order in the world. To do all we can to see heaven break into humanity. A woven compassion is the giving of oneself to this new social vision in all areas of life – to bring about a kingdom of equality, a social harmony, a heaven on earth, through our small everyday actions.

The island of Molokai witnessed such a heaven on earth. Amid the worst suffering of humanity, among the most dejected and abandoned people, through the work of this one priest, heaven, a new and just society, became a reality on the earth. Heaven found its dwelling in a leper colony, the most unexpected of places.

It is reported that in December 1884 Father Damien accidentally placed his foot into scalding water and realised that he did not feel pain as his skin blistered. After 16 years caring for these societal outcasts, he had finally contracted the disease. Years after declaring himself a leper in solidarity with his brothers and sisters, he had finally become one. During his final years, he kept working and serving and actually increased all he was doing to support those on the island.

During Holy Week, on 15 April 1889, at the age of 49, Father Damien died from the disease of leprosy.

~

Whoever really loves will use a magnifying glass to see the small and hidden details of another's need. I will be able to see that he has cold feet and I can move him nearer the fire; that he is deaf and I must speak closer to his ear; that a secret anxiety torments him; that he longs for a good word; and many more things which usually lie, seemingly hidden, under the surface of our lives.

Helmut Thielicke[75]

A Woven Faith

And faith – that changes too. It has to. It is a cardboard
kaleidoscope, ever turning and being turned … You have
learned that it is impossible to divide things neatly, and that
the second you begin to define something, you limit it … You
are finished with most of the raging now. There will still be
moments when someone says or does something that sparks
some hidden anger, and for a few moments you will rant
white-hot over a past spiritual wrong. But then it will flicker and
crumble away like ash … You are tired of wandering … You
could leave. There are a million reasons you could come up
with to leave. But you decide, for now, to stay.

Addie Zierman[76]

Vomit and poo and a mundane existence

I talk a lot more about vomit and poo than I ever used to. It is true. The
joy of parenting. A son's spew at 3 a.m. flowing through fingers in a
somewhat hopeless attempt to avoid changing a bedsheet for the fourth
time that night. Bucket lying somewhere on the floor. My pregnant wife
throwing up in the room next door. The next morning our son is feeling
fine and now playing pretend. He holds up the bucket and fakes a vomit.
Just like mum does. He is proud of the joke and laughs his head off as
he does so.

This is who I have become, I think to myself. Vomit and poo. They are a
consistency in my life. Often more than writing and poetry. Often more
than connecting with God.

And if it's not these bodily explosions then it's hour upon hour of
reading the same book over and over. That damn hungry little caterpillar
has eaten through a planet's worth of food by now. And there can be no
lying down for more than 10 seconds before being pulled up from the
couch to play games and to chase the boy around the house. And it's one

more load of washing, and the lawn that needs mowing, and dirty dishes in the sink, and this playground followed by that one, and a crying son, and counting down the hours till mum gets home. And this – this is life. All this is life.

The mundane kicks you sometimes. In the face. Hard.

And I don't just see it in my life as a parent. It is there for us all. Behind the Instagram photo and the Facebook post lies reality. Mundane reality. Vomit and poo. We spend our lives running from it, but it's always going to be there. Even for the full-time poet, or the famous singer, or the actor, or the travel photographer or (insert any glamourised vocation). Life is filled with the mundane. So I figure we might as well own up to it. Are you ready?

Your life is not that exciting.

Sure, there are moments of exhilaration worthy of the movies. But most of the time it's working hard and cleaning dishes and answering emails and dealing with annoying people and problems with your bowels and a friend who is depressed. And it's eating and pooing and buying groceries and getting sick and coping with insect bites and self-doubt and crippling loneliness and suffocating families and watching countless hours of TV. There is no escape. Everyone. Everywhere. We are all faced with the mundane.

Life can be so darn ... boring.

Yet I wonder if these mundane realities are actually where faith finds its footing – a woven faith that looks past the profane to see the sacred in everything. I wonder if boredom comes only when we give ourselves to it. I wonder if boredom comes because we have lost our sense of wonder. Boredom is the curse of a generation that has been given too much.

So could I find wonder still at 3 am cleaning up vomit?

Could I find God in the present reality of my mundane existence? I am sure God must be there.

Possibly I might find the wonder in the knowing that I have a child, and this child looks like me, and the love that I feel for him is something unexplainable. And I know so many people who cannot have children for one reason or another and how blessed I am, actually, that I can clean up his vomit. And if need be, I can take him to the doctors when so many sick children in the world do not have access to medicine. This is life. Beneath all the mundane and all that we are tempted to be bored with and escape from, I do wonder if there is always more to it.

The Woven is a lived experience of the Divine. It may not look like the on-fire, passionate, emotional, 'being-in-love' experience of my teenage evangelical faith. Coming into the Woven is not about the feeling of a passion that was. For I am simply not the person that was. What once was cannot be again.

Rather, the passion I have found is something much deeper. It runs inside, beneath feelings. Occasionally my emotions tap into this river for a short time, but this lived experience of faith is far beyond emotion. It is not an escape from 'normal' life into something spiritual, as the emotional God experiences of my teenage life often were. Rather, it is to find the spiritual *in* the normal. The Divine in what looks much more like real life. It is to experience God in the silence, in the noise, in the washing of dishes, in the talking with friends, in the walking along the sand. The sacred hides beneath reality. There are no mundane moments, if we have the eyes to see.

As Paula D'Arcy states, 'God comes to you disguised as your life.'[77]

The grass always seems to be greener on the other side of the fence of our lives. But it never is. Faith is not greener over there. It would not be greener if only I were more faithful, if only I felt the fire of my teenage passion like I once did. If only ... If only ...

You do not need to run from this, from who you are. The Unravelled Self believed the invitation was to flee to somewhere other. The Woven Self realises that *who you are* will always follow you, and that the invitation is not to flee this person but to learn to embrace them.

So let the rope you once thought tied you down be the very anchor that holds you in the midst of storm and circumstance.

Let me say that again.

Let the rope you once thought tied you down be the very anchor that holds you in the midst of storm and circumstance.

Too much of our existence is lost through our inattention to the things that matter. We get caught up in the chaos and so lose the deeper sense of life and our connection to it. By our choice to slow down, to reconnect, our small lives are woven in with the breadth of life offered to us by the world. We give our sacred selves into the gentle hands of the present moment. You have one life, and that life is lived in the present. There is no 'if only'. There is only you and this present moment. It is just one of a trillion, yet it is the one that matters. Our ability to choose is only ever found in the moment we find ourselves in. It is a microscopic picture of our macro lives.

It may not be the life you wish for, nor the life you hoped for, nor the life you thought you would have. But it is this life. Right now. Right here. *Your* life, just as it is. God comes to you within your life, when you least expect it. Always coming, always going. Always flirting, always coaxing. It is the weaving of everyday experience and the sacred, the threading of the common with the eternal.

What if God is a child hiding badly in a game of hide-and-seek, her foot showing from behind the curtains of our everyday? The laugh of my child. The birds that fly overhead. The touch of my wife. God in the mundane. There she is. Peek-a-boo.

A woven faith is a movement towards living with intentionality. It is faith not as a system of articulated belief and doctrine but as the reality of everyday life hung upon something larger. Such intentionality is seen in the Jewish concept of *kavanah*,[78] which, as Jewish philosopher Martin Buber writes, is the quality displayed by someone who 'completes an act in such a way that his whole existence is gathered in it and directed in it towards God'.[79] It is a choice to take the trivial and the tension and the broken relationship and the bung knee and the feeling of shame and the changing of nappies and to weave all of these into the larger reality that is God and his dream for the world.

Let us delve beneath the facade of the self we want to project to everybody else and no longer seek to escape from the mundane reality we find beneath it. Let us see if somewhere in the midst of it all we can find the wonder again. The grass is not greener on the other side, so let us find meaning in the mundane. Beauty in the boring. Enchantment in the everyday. Positivity in the poo (OK, that may be taking it too far). Here's to life in all its glory and all its ordinary. I'll see you there, in the midst of it all, probably with red tired eyes and vomit stains on my shirt. I'll see you there, where faith finds its footing.

Bricklaying

A man was walking down a road. Let's call him Geoffrey. In his walk, Geoffrey happened upon a building site. He strolled alongside it and saw a man laying bricks.

Being an inquisitive fellow, Geoffrey walked over and asked, 'What are you up to?'

The man replied flatly, 'Me? Not much. Nothing at all really. Just this unbelievably boring job. One brick after another after another. This is the worst! Jobs like this take forever.'

'Ah, I am sorry to hear that,' replied Geoffrey as he said goodbye.

He continued on his way down the path beside the building site until he came across another man who was also laying bricks. Geoffrey was a curious fellow indeed, so he asked the second man the same question, 'Hey mate, what you are you up to?'

'Hi there,' replied the second bricklayer, looking up from his work. With a little more enthusiasm than the first man, he answered, 'Well, we're building a wall here. My job is laying the bricks. A few of us are assigned to build this thing; it starts down that way where my friend is and ends a fair way back up where you came from. It's going to be pretty high by the time we're done, I can tell you!'

Geoffrey thanked the second labourer for his time and walked on down the path a little further. He came across a third bricklayer and, true to fashion, walked up to the man and asked, 'Hello there. What are you up to?'

The third man looked up from his work with a smile and a glint in his eye. In a torrent of enthusiasm he replied, 'Mate, you should see what we're building!' He swung his arms up above his head, motioning to the entire building site. 'This is just one part of a huge cathedral. It's going to be absolutely stunning. There's a massive team of people all over the site constructing the different sections. I've never worked on anything so … so epic before. Wait …' He paused and reached behind himself to pull out some large rolls of paper. 'You just have a look at these blueprints! There are four turrets around the main nave, the narthex comes down to here and …' The man continued on, talking to Geoffrey about the glories of the cathedral for quite some time.

We are all bricklayers. We are all caught up in the reality of the mundane life. There are so many bricks to be laid in our lifetime. As much as we may want a thrilling life of adventure, the reality is we will never escape from the wearisome activities of life.

The question this fable puts to us is, what kind of bricklayer will we be? What will be our posture towards the normality of life?

The fable speaks to the perspective, the intent, that we bring into our realities. It affirms the idea that our way of seeing things changes everything about how we engage with those things.

The first bricklayer could not see beyond his own perspective. He missed the big picture. He forgot the intent. He simply gave himself over to the soul-crushing work he believed bricklaying to be. A monotonous, weary existence. It wouldn't surprise me if he gave up his job and went looking for something more exciting somewhere else, only to find the mundane there also.

The second man saw something more and so enjoyed his work more. He knew he was not alone, that other builders were around him. He could picture the wall being built.

The third had the whole grand cathedral in mind. A focus of intent. He knew how small things lead to big things. He knew he was contributing as one of a large group of workers. A much larger story shaped the posture by which he worked, and this made all the difference.

Three men doing the same thing. Three very different ways of being with their work.

The bricklayers' actions were identical; the difference lay in the intent that sat beneath those actions. This difference in perspective changed nothing of what they were actually doing, yet it changed everything.

In the spiritual journey, it is not that our movement forward means we no longer have the routine, ordinary, boring tasks of our lives to complete. There is still dishes to be washed, lawns to mow, bricks to lay. However, as our context is woven into something larger, these small everyday actions make much more sense.

From laying bricks to building cathedrals.

From living out of our small stories to giving ourselves to a larger story.

Nothing changes and yet everything changes.

This is a woven faith.

> Chop wood. Carry water. Enlightenment. Then ...
> Chop Wood. Carry Water.
>
> **Zen Proverb**

Living by a rhythm

Every morning the growing dawn opens its arms to the promise of a new day. By dusk, the sky is once again stained red with its memory. The morning is a time of invitation, of unfolding into the light. The evening is a time of drawing back inwards, taking into oneself the day that has been.

As the falling sun draws into itself all the vibrancy and colour of the earth, so we too draw the day into the reflective space within. We hold the colour within us as the world turns into grey and black night. We hold the day until sleep greets us – until we once again become open armed and surrendered in our slumber. We let go of the day in the dreams of the night ... only to arrive empty on the shore of tomorrow ready to be taken back into the promises of a new day and all that will fill us in the light.

This cyclical movement of drawing in and letting out, of embracing and letting go, of soaking into us the experiences of the day and letting them go in the release of sleep – we are always being called back into this rhythm.

The daytime rhythm of action and unfolding
>   of interactions and relationships
>   of activity and projects
>   of being drawn out of oneself to give to the world.
The evening rhythm of inward movements
>   of embracing and reflecting
>   of sorting and sifting
>   of drawing one's energy into the heart space where
>   we are recreated
>   of letting go of control.
The way of activism. The way of surrender.

We are a cyclical people. A people of rhythm. The problem is that we are not intentional about the patterns by which we live, especially in regard to faith.

We live by rhythms whether we like it or not. Often these are not healthy rhythms. They are rhythms of avoidance, rhythms built around doing anything but reflecting and delving inward. We lose our balance. The apathetic who stay sleeping too long. The workaholics who live too many hours in the light of day. The self-absorbed who do not give of themselves to others but get stuck in a room full of mirrors.

We are creatures of pattern. These patterns quickly become habits. These habits are the rhythms by which we live.

We cannot escape this life of patterns, habits and rhythms, so we must intentionally choose the ones we want to follow. If we do not choose a way of life for ourselves then one will be chosen for us. This choosing will most often be done by our Western Dream society that idolises progress and performance. If we do not shape our own existence, it will be shaped by others.

So look at your hands and at those things you have found yourself still carrying. Those convictions that became truth and life for you when all else fell away. Begin with these. What would it look like to live these out in your life? What actions, patterns, rhythms might be linked to

185

them? These things are what you now shape your life around.

The childhood life is shaped by external rules – by schools and parents and authority figures telling us what to do. As we enter adulthood, these external rules no longer apply. The adult life must be shaped by something *other*. It must flow from the internal, from one's chosen values and convictions. Living into who we desire to become will always require intentionality. We must purposefully step into the rhythms that will get us there. A woven way of life weaves our convictions with the values we hold and the everyday actions we engage in, our personal beliefs with our social existence.

It is here that faith is built on consciously chosen commitments and so becomes owned and integrated and intentional and explicit.

This why we need to come to attention about the deep places within, for it is out of these places that the rest of our life will flow.

~

I have a friend named Stephanie who has been knitting for many years. She takes her needles with her wherever she goes. She knits in meetings and movies and conversations. She knits because that is how her hands move. Steph makes knitting look easy.

My wife makes it look hard. A slow and sometimes frustrating process, as is often the case when we start a new venture. She takes steps with care and precision. Her knitting is two stitches forward, one stitch back. It is mistake and losing the thread; it is focus and concentration.

Fingers slowly learn these new movements. Movements that will become habit. Habit that will become rhythm.

With lots of practice, my wife will one day knit like my friend Steph. She will move from methodical steps consciously enacted to a place where the movement simply happens through her fingers without the need for direct cognitive choice. It is here the stitches will be gathered together in new patterns – not by the determined effort of the knitter but by the rhythm they have given themselves to. Needles will click together in high speed movements until a beautiful form grows almost organically.

What appears as graceful will have come about through long hours of hard work.

186

We all start this way: this slow weaving. The focused attention of a woven way of faith. Two steps forward, one step back. Mistakes made and a frustration with who we wish we were already. We choose the practices – or more likely, they choose us – and we try them out again and again, over and over, until they are part of us. Until our chosen commitments flow out into beautiful patterns. We build our life anew from the foundations up, slowly.

By these practices, by this rhythm, we are held.

When all you believe is lost and you are lost and God is lost, it is these rhythms, these patterns, these actions, that may be the very things to carry you forward.

Or perhaps they won't … and this is OK too. Failure is OK.

Please hear me: I am not saying that everything will be fine if you can shape your life around intentional rhythms. This is not THE answer. This is simply a way to walk differently to what you have been doing. It is a way to hold together the threads.

~

What are the deep *convictions* of your life?

What are the *values* that flow out of these convictions?

What are the *practices* that then come from these values?

This is the way we bring our lives into a new rhythm: threading our convictions together with our values and our actions. This is the way we weave together our faith with the daily practices of our lives.

So make a list: a list of your convictions.

Make another list: a list of the practices you already see playing out in your life.

Take the list of convictions and name the value that stems from each one, and then name some identifiable practices you will commit to practising until they become a rhythm.

Take the list of practices you already engage in and ask: do the rhythms you already live by stem from your stated convictions, or are they incongruous? For instance, if a core conviction of yours is 'life is short, make the most of it', yet a rhythm you see in your life is how much time you waste on social media or watching TV, then this shows a dissonance between your rhetoric and your reality. It shows you what your life is calling you to change.

~

And then there is the grace

True spirituality will never be about perfecting oneself through moralism and correct doctrine, actions and right behaviour. True spirituality is not about the performance mentality that so shaped my evangelical upbringing as well as my rebellion against it. True spirituality is not a quest to be the best we can be in spite of our brokenness. True spirituality is never 'in spite of our brokenness.' The Divine meets us always in the middle of our mess. Right in the middle of our fumbling attempts. Right in the middle of the gap between who we are and who we desire to be. The Divine sits in this place with us.

Every time I desire growth in who I am, every time I move forward, the very next moment I find myself moving backward. I act out in love only to moments later act out in selfishness. I give of myself and then the next day am twice as tight-fisted as ever. Or I give without realising I am just trying to prove myself, to butter up my own ego. I honour the beauty in someone only to turn my head and objectify someone else. I act from love, I lie back in apathy.

In all this, still the Divine meets me. Not in spite of these realities, but rather within these realities.

True spirituality, then, is a surrender of our need to be perfect. It is a self-emptying of the standards we hold up and can never reach. It is a falling back into grace – a graciousness given to myself leading to Divine graciousness. Or perhaps it is the other way around. The chicken and egg of grace and forgiveness. It is to let yourself off the hook. It is to *be* let off the hook.

Too much religion upholds a spirituality of ascent, of moving upward towards perfection. The pressure to perform. Religious people are often on about doing what they can to reach God. We reach higher and higher by our acts of moralism. We build our Babels in the sky because we think God resides there. Yet while we are seeking to move ever upward in our spirituality, the Divine is, in fact, on his way down.

A journey to perfection is the complete opposite to the journey of spiritual formation. One is a thorough building up of the ego; the other is a surrender. It is what Mike Yaconelli calls a 'messy spirituality'[80] – to choose to sit in the wounds that lie beneath our destructive patterns and to invite the Divine, and others, into that place. And to know you are not rejected in that place. You are not accepted *in spite of* such brokenness; rather, you are embraced in the midst of it, through it, within it. This is the movement of descent – the movement of surrender.

The way forward, then, cannot lie in the disregarding and discarding of the brokenness. Such a feat is impossible. The way forward lies not in the rejection of it but the acceptance of it, the befriending of it, and the subsequent transformation and integration of it.

We have a deep tendency to loathe our weakness, recoil from our brokenness, escape the messiness. Then, as we are busy proving ourselves by how together we are, by how *spiritual* we are, the Divine bypasses our ego and wraps around the fear and the wound and the thorn and the poverty.

We run *from* the wound; the Divine runs *into* the wound. The Divine embraces the human condition where it is most frail and says, 'You are OK, even here.' There should be no shame. No self-hatred. No condemnation. Just grace.

Grace. That which makes beauty out of ugliness.

Grace. A radical self-acceptance.

Grace. A love that is so much larger than requirement.

Grace transforms all it touches.

~

An old friend of mine once told me that his favourite time of the week was washing his car with his little boy. They would pull out the buckets and soap and sponges and get to work. The problem was that inevitably the little boy would drop the sponge onto the ground. Not being old enough to understand, he would then continue washing the car with the dirty sponge. Looking up to his dad, he would say, 'Look at me, Dad! Look how amazing I am at washing the car!'

The car never got cleaner when it was washed by this little boy. A job that could have taken a short time took longer. This could have been an absolute pain for my friend, yet he would say, 'I wouldn't have it any other way.'

The point was not that the car became ultra-clean; the point was that they got to do this together. The mess was not important. It was just father and son, and that is what mattered.

I sometimes wonder if all my attempts at making a better world, at becoming a better person, at trying to change lives, are all nothing more than a little boy with a dirty sponge muddying a car while looking up and saying, 'Look at me, God! Look at what a great job I'm doing!'

And the truly beautiful thing is that I hear the Divine saying back, 'I wouldn't have it any other way, son. I wouldn't have it any other way.'

A Woven Truth

For everything, absolutely everything, above and below, visible and invisible, rank after rank after rank of angels – *everything* got started in him and finds its purpose in him. He was there before any of it came into existence and holds it all together right up to this moment. And when it comes to the church, he organizes and holds it together, like a head does a body.

Colossians 1:16-17[81]

This river-speak

The valley was black. Charcoal. Stripped bare and made ash. Green turned red turned ember turned cinder turned death.

I drove down its length, my car piled full of tent and food, headed into the bush for a weekend all by myself. A needed retreat.

I had driven to the hills, not really knowing where I would end up, just moving until it felt right. The crest of a hill gave way to this valley and suddenly the green leaves and brown trees turned black.

It had been a year since bushfires had swept through this area. The fires were some of the worst the state of Victoria had ever seen. Houses had been destroyed and lives taken, and we had watched the tragedy unfolding on our TVs. The billowing smoke. The world aflame. A friend lost his uncle. My cousins lost their home. They called it Black Saturday.

Now a year later I drove down the dirt-track spine of the valley. Once again it was summer, and a searing heat haze sat over the charred remains. The scorched ground of despair birthed from the ferocity of nature.

Yet as I drove deeper into it, something began to change. Amid the black, I saw green. Small flecks of it. Tiny shoots bursting through the ash. Wiry green grass splitting the black soil. Sprouts pushing out from their coating of death to grow from the branches of a tree.

I turned the corner as I reached the floor of the valley and saw the

191

source from which all these had found life again. The Murrindindi River. It meandered its way along the valley floor, glistening bright on the sunny day. An invitation.

I pulled the car over and walked down to the river. 'River' is a generous word – it was more like a creek at this point. I walked along its edge and looked closely at the new life germinating by its banks. I bent low and placed my hand in the cool water. Another invitation. Another whisper.

I knew somewhere inside that I had to get into the river. There was no reason why. I did not have any swimming clothes on, and the little creek certainly wasn't the sort of place you would just go for a swim. The surrounds were a broken, blackened husk with nothing like an enticing waterhole to be seen. But the whisper was there.

As I stood on the edge of the river, I thought of the people who had lost their lives and houses to the fire. I thought, too, of the times of deep burning in my own life, when the inside valleys were stripped bare and laid waste. The times I lost myself and could not breathe in the haze and smoke. I had taken the personal retreat on this weekend because now was such a time. The demands of a busy life had left me hung out and dry. Too dry. Parched and scorched and decimated. I had come seeking solace from the relentlessness of people and their problems. It seemed I had lost God somewhere in it all. His absence had become obvious.

Inside, too, was a black valley, carved too deep. Who knew the burnt and brittle inside could look so much like the outside?

I dipped a toe in the water. Took off my shirt. Stepped out into the river. It was up to my knees at its deepest. I kneeled down and folded my legs, moulding them into the sand and stones. I felt the rush of fresh water up to my stomach, the exhilaration of coolness on a hot day. A flow of life in the midst of a valley of death. Kneeling there, I thought of death and life and how the two are inseparable. I let the water cleanse me and wash away the burnt parts. Tears fell from my face to join the rush of the river. Fresh water tasting salt.

Then I placed my whole self under the water. I leaned forward until I was completely submerged by the stream. Holding my breath. I let the water flow over me and wash away the ash and death inside. A baptism.

A new beginning. Resurrection.

Immersed into the heart of the world, I was not just dunking in a creek in that moment. I was plunged into the great river from which all streams flow. There is a wellspring of wisdom hidden in the valleys and streams of the natural world – a wisdom too easily missed, for we shrink wisdom down to knowledge and knowledge down to a cognitive appropriation of facts. This was a far different wisdom, a deeper truth. This river-knowing was something greater.

I had not realised that rivers could speak. This one did.

I floated in her waters and she told me of the day the fires came. She spoke of how she had been here through it all. As the smoke drifted in on the wind. As the flames crept over the edge of the valley. As the trees raged with fire. As the world around was scorched and burnt and left for dead. She was here in the barren ash of a world that was no more. She carried life deep in her bosom in this place that had been so stripped bare. In her the pain of the earth met its rebirth.

She spoke as well to the burnt-out valleys inside my inner world. 'A river shall always run through it,' she said. 'A stream of life present in the darkest season. Even when it cannot be seen, it flows, deeper and deeper, seeking out the arid places. Stirring something once lost and forgotten. The green will come again. Just as I am bringing life back to this valley, the green will come again.'

By her words, I felt the green spring up through the black ash of my inner landscape. I felt as one with her, this river, this truth.

~

This river-speak. This river-knowing. There is no other way I could have learned this truth as I needed to. No textbook. No dictionary. No sermon. No words of someone else that could have done inside what this immersion in a river did.

Science would tell me that a river does not speak. I would tell science there is a knowing far greater than such deduction.

The things of spirit can never be reduced to the rational brain and our ability to engage in logical reasoning. God is present where we so often deem God not to be. God is speaking through burning bushes and rushing rivers and burnt-out valleys. Beauty breaks through the veil of normality to whisper in such fleeting moments. God is beauty. God is love. Should we choose to open our eyes, to be present, to slow down, we can see truth for what it is.

Even as you read of this river experience and glean from it for your own life, I would say that unless you actually put yourself in the river, unless you feel the ash and the water and the death and resurrection, then the truth that found me on that day cannot be fully known by you. Truth is a shy friend. I can tell you all about her, but until you meet her, until you rub shoulders with her and let her touch you, until you are immersed in her flow, you cannot truly know her.

A head-knowing of truth falls far short of a true knowing. To know a thing is to be known by a thing – to experience the depths of it within your own depths.

We have sacrificed this knowing for a scientific, cognitive form of knowledge. It was the Enlightenment that produced this bias towards the rational, in a backlash against the superstitious religious world of the Middle Ages. Our ability to deduce became the focal point of the scientific revolution. All knowledge was reduced to the cognitive process of reason – put forth a hypothesis and then logically analyse it to come to a rational conclusion.

True things of spirit, however, can never be reduced to the rational brain. By elevating our ability to engage in logical deductions, we have missed out on a knowing that comes from the weaving together of experience and truth. We can know a thing in a way that cannot be reduced to reason.

This difference in knowing is the difference between studying the chemical make-up of chocolate and placing a piece of chocolate on your tongue and letting it melt inside your mouth. It is the difference between looking at photographs of the Sistine Chapel and actually being there, gazing till your neck is sore but not being able to look away. It is the difference between knowing the mechanics of having sex and the complete giving of yourself, in the ecstasy of the moment, to the smell and curves of another. It is the difference between reading about a mountain on Wikipedia and standing atop a mountain feeling the rush of cold air through your lungs. It is the difference between studying a river and letting her speak to you.

John Keats said, 'Nothing ever becomes real till it is experienced.'[82]

The facts of a thing do not tell us everything about that thing. We may chase the facts and still miss the truth – especially in regards to spiritual things. If knowledge is going to last within us, it should be a knowledge that is tangible and textured. It should rub between finger and thumb. It should get caught at the back of your throat when a sunset stares through you. It should leave you speechless because there is no speaking that can communicate it.

This knowing is a participatory knowing – a knowing you can smell and taste. It is an aesthetic knowing. It is a knowing that comes through slowing down and looking once more around you. It is an embodied knowing, finding its way within you as you move out into the flow of the world and open your life up to where it is speaking. This knowing is thoroughly woven in with the world around.

~

Contemplation is a sudden gift of awareness, an awakening to the Real within all that is real.

Thomas Merton[83]

A mystic I could follow

Two hours after my self-imposed dunk in the Murrindindi River, I said goodbye to the waters and drove away, up and out of the charcoal valley. The water had done its work and I breathed easier as I drove. I felt lighter. I wound down the windows and let the wind come at me.

I was a new man, and I still had a whole weekend to re-find myself. But first I needed to find somewhere to set up a tent, and before that I needed some gas for the camp stove. I drove through a large town and took my gas bottle to the petrol station. But my gas bottle was old and the connection would not fit. I went from shop to shop around town trying to find another connection, and what was supposed to be a five-minute stop took me 90 minutes.

One hour after leaving the river, I had well and truly lost her peace. Frustration had taken over. I lost my temper and cursed the gas bottle again and again. No one was there to care.

After finally fitting the gas bottle with the right connection, I headed off to find a camping spot. I had been told about a place called Big Pat's Creek, about half an hour from where I was, so I drove in that direction. As I took to the road, I thought I would check out some other places along the way. I stopped a few times but none of them met my expectations for a weekend retreat. So I kept driving. I came to Big Pat's Creek but decided to drive on, just to see if there was anything better. No success. I started getting frustrated again, telling myself I should just go back to Big Pat's Creek. And yet it was as though I couldn't let go of the thought that maybe, just around the corner, would be *the* perfect spot. My FOMO had taken over. I turned my frustration inward and cursed myself and my indecision.

Finally, I pounded my fist against the steering wheel, turned the car around and headed back to Big Pat's Creek. Again, I was fuming. Twice already on a supposed 'spiritual retreat' I had found myself lost in a negative space. My thoughts turned to self-judgement about ever having the spiritual depth I so desired. I ripped into myself for failing already on this weekend away. The harsh inward gaze.

Bathed in the afternoon sun, I walked down the path into Big Pat's Creek. I turned a corner and there was the spot I had so desired: a beautiful grassy patch right beside a little creek, away from the valleys burnt by fire and under a lush rainforest canopy. No one else was around.

I set up the tent. The creek gurgled at me, the echoing voice of the river that had spoken to me earlier that day. I finished setting up and sat on top of a fallen log that spanned the water. I took off my shoes and rubbed my toes on the green moss of the log, then dropped my feet to dangle in the water. And I pulled out the only book I had brought with me for the retreat: the collected personal diaries of Thomas Merton, a Trappist monk.

I spent the next few days with Merton. Or that is what it felt like. Merton and me in the garden. I soaked in his words, poetic and personal. I immersed myself in the heart of this great mystic. And I was utterly surprised at how ordinary he was – how he, too, never lived up to how 'spiritual' he wanted to be. How confused he was, and how he also looked too harshly inwards.

When we think of a mystic, we often think of a monk who lives in a cave atop a high mountain. Lost in a spiritual world, he floats above the earth in a transcendent experience the rest of us can only wish we had the patience for. While I would not seek to critique the practice of such a monk, I found another form of mysticism in Merton. His was a mysticism for the rest of us. An earthed spirituality. The myth of Merton may be that of a spiritual guru floating above the earth, but the man Merton I encountered in his diaries was a gentle, fallible, broken man seeking to commune with the Divine in the setting sun and the changing seasons and the everyday strokes of life.

The myth and the man – I'll take the man any day. He makes me feel like my own stumbling, bumbling ways are somehow ... legitimate. That it is OK when I miss the mark.

After 22 years as a monk, only four years before his death, on 22 February 1964, Merton the man wrote in his diary:

> In all sobriety and honesty I must admit that the twenty-two years have not been well spent ... twenty-two years of relative confusion, often coming close to doubt and infidelity, agonised aspirations for *something better*, criticism of what I have, inexplicable inner suffering that is largely my own fault, insufficient efforts to overcome myself, inability to find my way.[84]

And again, two years later, on 5 September 1966:

> I will probably go on like this for the rest of my life. Here I am – this patchwork, this bundle of questions and doubts and obsessions, this gravitation to silence and to the woods and to love. This incoherence!![85]

Merton was a mystic I could follow. A woven patchwork. Another time, on 25 August 1965, he wrote in his journal of his everyday form of spirituality:

> The blessing of sawing wood, cutting grass, cleaning house, washing dishes. The blessing of a quiet, alert, concentrated, fully 'present' meditation. The blessing of God's presence and guidance.[86]

Evelyn Underhill was another great contemporary mystic of a similar vein. In her book *Practical Mysticism for Normal People*, she says, 'Mysticism is the art of union with reality.'[87] It is not reaching for a place that is totally other and transcendent. It is connecting with the other and the transcendent in *this* place, in the midst of the normality, boredom and frustration of life. Spirit is woven in with the grass and the dirt we walk on, and with artworks and relationships and ball games and food, and all those things that are so … earthy. So ordinary. So everyday.

A friend of mine, who has a very eclectic spirituality, once told me she had a dream of Jesus. In the dream Jesus came to her in the night. He was floating above the ground, and she found herself getting angry about this. She took some paint and a brush and began to paint Jesus down to the ground so that he was no longer floating above it. As she finished painting, this grounded Jesus morphed into a tree.

I like this dream. I like a Jesus who is connected to the earth, not one who floats above it. I like a spirituality that does not run from the earth but is woven in with it. I like a Christianity that finds God and thus also finds the self in the ordinary reality of life and circumstance.

As the sun went down that night by the creek, the clouds came over and it started to rain. I sat under the tarpaulin pulled down over the front of my tent and lit a few candles, watching them chase away the dark. I watched the bugs too – they saw the candlelight and, as is their way, came closer and closer. The light too addictive, they did not realise the danger. One after another, burnt dead bugs fell into the pooling wax of the red candle. Couldn't they see their fixation was killing them?

I pitied them, until I saw myself in them.

My fixations. The expectations I hold and can't seem to let go of. Gas-bottle stops that are meant to take five minutes. Not wanting to miss out on the perfect camping spot. My compulsions.

I blew out the candle as a prayer. And as I sat there by Big Pat's Creek, I finally came to the point of truly looking at my inner life. Contemplation does this. An awareness of the outer world, a slowing down, leads us into the truth of the inner world. The weave of the inner and the outer.

~

To find the sacred within I must cultivate the proper eyes with which to see the world.

Frank MacEowen[88]

I like the idea of this, of slowing down to be present. But the reality is that I have a problem with this way of attentiveness, this waiting. My problem is that I cannot stop. I must constantly be productive or I do not feel as though I am doing enough.

I am a driven, entrepreneurial type. A leader. A pioneer. Constantly moving and challenging myself with a new goal. I am a very passionate person and give my whole self to whatever I am engaged in. A three on the Enneagram. This is both one of my great strengths and one of my great weaknesses.

The other things in my life – other tasks, other people – all fall to the periphery. Such blindness on my part has led to the fracturing of friendships, to disappointment, to burnout. I run the world and miss the point. And even when I am forced to slow down to wait for something, it is never a present waiting. Too often I wait distracted and burdened and stacked back and folding over. The crossed arms across the chest. The pacing thoughts and itchy skin. The 'I can't wait to be doing something useful again.' This is not awareness and presence.

I have never been taught how to do this waiting well. Never present, never holding. Just pace – the feet movement and the blur. I cannot abide the silence, so I hide from it in gadgets and distractions. In the iPhone. In the noise. I am filled with earwax, filled with static – a radio tuned out. I do not listen to the inner voice.

But oh, to bend inward! Not the concave bend of being forced down, but turning in towards the desolate and the whispered and the unresolved and the left behind. Holding hands with the silent one who sits waiting inside and hoping, always hoping, that I will come to his chapel home. Knock on the door. Offer myself on the altar. Learn this way of breathing and stretching, and find that inside is far more spacious than it looks. All Tardis and larger. All infinite.

Push the walls back. Melt into this. Listen. Wait. The deeper inside, the deeper outside.

~

> The time of business does not with me differ from the time of prayer; and in the noise and clatter of my kitchen, while several persons are at the same time calling for different things, I possess God in as great tranquility as if I were upon my knees at the blessed sacrament ... I keep myself by a simple attention, and a general fond regard to God, which I may call an actual presence of God; or, to speak better, an habitual, silent and secret conversation of the soul with God, which often causes me joy and raptures inwardly and sometimes also outwardly ... As for my set hours of prayer, they are only a continuation.
>
> **Brother Lawrence**[89]

Tree-hugging hippy

Early the next morning I left Merton and the bug-graveyard candle behind as I crossed Big Pat's Creek and found a path. It led away from my little campsite and deeper into the surrounding woods. Mist gathered thick and brooding among the trees, waiting for the morning sunrise to heat the world.

I walked the path. My walk turned to thoughts – thoughts once again of this earthy mysticism, of talkative rivers in burnt-out valleys, of brother Merton, of how far my own everyday life seemed to be from a contemplative, woven way of being in the world.

I walked the path and realised again the depth of my problem. I have spent a lot of time among leaders and social activists, and I see the same shadow of busyness playing out for many of them. There is so much *doing* and so little *being*. Social action without self-reflection.

Leading people without leading the self. Social activists acting more out of unravelled anger towards the system than a genuine love for the people abused by the system.

There is a contemplative community in Victoria called the Community of the Transfiguration. One of the values they uphold at the centre of their communal life has been that, to breathe peace into the world, to disarm the world, you must first disarm your own heart.

Perhaps, in our current world, this slowing down, this self-reflection, this contemplation could be one of the most radical activities of all. Its veracity lies in its opposition to the constant drumming up of productivity and excessive busyness entrenched in Western society. The more we engage in lifestyles of activism, the more we must be people of contemplation. Our social influence inevitably flows out of our inner state of existence.

Jean Vanier says, 'It is only to the extent that we nurture our own hearts that we can keep interior freedom. People who are hyperactive, fleeing from their deep selves and their wound, become tyrannical and their exercise of responsibility becomes intolerable, creating nothing but conflict.'[90]

The further I went on the path that day, the denser the woods became. The heat of the previous day had turned overnight to chill and goose bumps. The path unfurled itself through the trees while the realisations of my life unfurled themselves within. I walked both paths at once. The depth of my problem with slowing down led to a frustration with myself which then led to the desire for change.

Right there, in the midst of my steps along the track, I made a firm commitment to learn how to be present to the world around. To teach my senses that they are spiritual. To thoroughly earth my spirituality. To learn how to wait in the silence and find the Divine already waiting for me.

~

Our perennial spiritual and psychological task is to look at things familiar until they become unfamiliar again.

G.K. Chesterton[91]

~

I chose to slow down my steps and to really look at the way the forest gathered itself around. I was mesmerised by it all. The carpet of green moss at my feet. The trickle of dew down the spine of a leaf. The pattern of the cracks in the clay. The roots that kissed the ground as a lover parting to cross the ocean. A bird's nest blown to the floor. The scurry of a lizard. The float of a blue butterfly. A deer looking on in elegant gait. The path ran off into the neglected places where the dark things creep. It untwisted itself into the wild places and the pine places and the ancient places.

The river had washed me clean the day before; the path now invited me forward. I walked with intention. Let the direction not matter, as long as I kept moving and seeing. This was the lesson: to walk forward with reflection, dawdle with contemplation, meander while paying attention. To be in this place in a different way, woven in with the life all around me. Listening to the ancient song that lingers.

In our world we are mostly deaf. There is a music that we do not hear because we are too busy to take notice. Too busy to take off our shoes. Too busy to know the within of things as well as the without. There is a tune that we have ceased to listen to. Thomas Moore calls this movement 'the re-enchantment of everyday life'[92] – the whisper that there is more to this life than what is before our eyes.

The forest path suddenly opened out at my feet and before me lay one of the largest gumtrees I had ever seen. It had fallen over, bent its knee into the end of its life. A grandfather finally resting. Its roots stood like a wall before me; torn from the earth, they towered above my reach. They also made a great ladder. I climbed the root system of the tree until I made it onto the huge fallen trunk of this ancient life. I walked its length, slowly. Then I lowered myself onto the old body and laid cheek to bark. Gumtrees can speak as loudly as rivers.

We sat and had a conversation, grandfather gumtree and me. We spoke about being present in the moment. About the longevity of a tree in its waiting. About the hyperactivity that overtakes me and the choice to slow down. We spoke of the changing of the seasons, of being rooted in the earth while still stretching out to the sky. The earth is an aged sage compared to the pimple-faced puberty of our short lives.

The Buddhist tradition speaks of this intentionality as the creation of mindfulness. Mindfulness is 'intentionally focusing one's attention on the experience occurring at the present time in an accepting way'.[93] It is a stepping back from the moment to observe the experience and bring an awareness of how the self is connected to it.

This mindfulness, this intentionality, is what we may even call prayer. For prayer, at its heart, is not about words and requests. It is an opening of oneself to the present moment and to the heart of the Divine within the present moment. It is a stilling of the mind, and an awakening to the sacredness of what is all around. The larger story. The sacrament of the present.

Saint Anthony of Egypt in the third century is reputed to have said, 'He prays best who does not know he is praying.' For if God is anything, then everything that is, is in God. Anywhere that love is present, God is also present. Contemplative prayer – or more, the contemplative lifestyle – is the opening up of oneself to the possibility of the Divine in one's every circumstance. Prayer is stepping forth into a deeper harmony with what is.

~

The contemplative self, then, is the self drawn into a lifestyle shaped by the subversive gentleness of the Divine presence. The contemplative are the artists who, in the place where they sit, listen for the whisper of its beauty and give themselves over to it. They lose themselves in this beauty to find themselves in this beauty. They are one with the moment, one with themselves, one with creation, one with the Divine. They are woven.

The spiritual movement is a movement towards oneness. It is not a journey about earning and entitlement but about discovering what we already hold within us. The very concept of grace upholds this at its core. Grace is a surrendering of our sense of separation and the walls that defend that sense. Our oneness with the Divine is not acquired; it is realised.

This woven oneness is the very essence of all that life is about. It is the constant theme that stems from the lives of the mystics through the ages and from the Christian Scriptures (John 14:20; 17:21; Galatians 2:19; Acts 17:28). We may be many, but we are one. This world may be made of many different things, but everything within it is one. God is separate, but God is also one.

Christian mystic Meister Eckhart said, 'The eye with which I see God is exactly the same eye with which God sees me.'[94]

Jesus said, 'I am in my Father, and you are in me, and I am in you' (John 14:20).

This is the great weaving. A weaving into oneness.

A community of truth

It must be said that such a weaving does also leave space for differentiation. There is individuality still. There remains a distinction between creator and creation, between me and you. As Peter Rollins says, we are not so much an indistinct waterdrop in the ocean of existence as a sponge on the bottom of the ocean. On the outside of the sponge is the ocean, and on the inside of the sponge is the ocean. The sponge is both held by the ocean and holds the ocean within itself. It is separate yet absolutely at one with the ocean.[95]

Such an understanding upholds what Martin Laird calls a 'differentiating union' where 'the more we realise we are one with God the more we become ourselves.'[96] We do not lose that which makes us 'us'. We do not lose our distinctiveness. Neither does the Divine. Rather, Laird writes, 'The creator is outpouring love, the creation, love outpoured.'[97] They are one and at the same time distinct. As Jesus says, 'I am the vine; you are the branches' (John 15:5).

The Sculpted demanded their truth statements as absolute – a position of power. The Unravelled sought to tear such power down, to disown all truth in the face of relativism. The danger with this in our individualist society is that we can end up with an outright indifference towards truth. Or we can end up with people claiming truth to be whatever they wish it to be, regardless of the effect this has on others. Thus, the leaders of our world state blatant lies and call them truth even when proved false. Thus, we have divisive social schisms.

The Woven Self has not let go of truth; it is not indifferent to truth.

Rather, it seeks to honour truth for what it is, something much larger than can ever be comprehended by an individual. The Woven hold that truth matters, especially in regard to social realities: the truth of human rights, the truth of justice, the truth of peace, the truth of love. These truths lie at the base of our common humanity.

In regards to the non-provable, to the spiritual, the Woven Self finds truth where truth is revealed. There the Woven has a dynamic relationship with truth – not needing to demand its answers are absolute but rather letting these truths change the Self. The spiritual is always beyond the factual – a truth that is a lived experience in the world of the Christ in whom all things 'live and move and have their being' (Acts 17:28).

So there I lay on the great fallen grandfather gumtree, and I wondered with it, and in my wondering I came to grasp truth. Perhaps not a scientific truth – at least not a propositional fact – but still, truth. I met with God in this truth. I met with Christ. I met with myself.

In the face of the largeness of Truth, the Woven recognise their own smallness. Their inability to capture Truth. Yet they do not run the other way. They meet with and they dialogue. Dialogue with others. Dialogue with nature. Dialogue with self. Dialogue with society. Dialogue with Christ. Dialogue with the Scriptures. Dialogue with tradition. Dialogue with their ancestry. Dialogue with emotions. Dialogue with experience. Dialogue with the Spirit.

Truth is found in the interplay of these multiplicities, this inter-weave of perspective. A truth that is profoundly communal.

Indeed, the Woven, at its essence, is community: a community of truth, a community of belonging. One and yet distinct. It is no wonder that the Divine in the Christian faith is seen the same way. The concept of the Trinity is that God is three-in-one. One and yet distinct. It is a truth that defies logic and reason, a truth far larger than the language we use to speak of it. But at its heart it is the truth that God is, in essence, relationship.

Father. Son. Spirit. A dance we are invited into. A community of undefinable truth where we are woven in with the great mystery that is God.

This, in the end, is the actual invitation. This is what the journey has been beckoning us to: the mystery that is God. To know the Divine, to know the self, to know the other, to know the earth. To be known by the Divine, to be known by the self, to be known by the other, to be known by the earth. This is truth. It is the invitation to relationship. It is the invitation to lifelong formation.

This is what I hold on to. This is where my hope lies. The invitation to the mystery. *There must be more than this.*

This is what causes me to keep going in this walk.

This is what keeps me living out my Christianity.

This is what keeps me challenging my Christianity.

This is what keeps me wrestling with the Scriptures.

This is what keeps me pursuing relationship with God, self, others, creation.

This is what keeps me discovering what faith may look like, and what truth may look like.

This is what keeps me journeying with a faith-community, opening myself up to the people around me.

This is what keeps me choosing to slow down and be present.

This is what keeps me challenging what my lifestyle may look like.

This is what keeps me naming my own prejudice and entitlement.

This is what keeps me shaping my life around a new rhythm.

This is what I hold on to: the depth of the mystery of God.

Do Not Despair

There is too much pain here. Have you seen it?
  Or not seen it as much as felt it.
  Let the broken wrap around you like chain.
Like heavy chain. Like Sorrow.

There is too much sorrow here.

  It gets under your skin,
          changes the way you feel,
  gets under your eyes,
          changes the way you see.
A dark lens and everything seems hopeless these days.
Everything seems hopeless.

  The little girls taken as sex slaves;
  The suicide behind detention centre fences;
  The black man shot; the little boy washed up on the beach;
  The wife beaten; the president and his grabby hands;
  The incarceration of colour;
  The starving children, always the starving children.

Despair is an absence
and I feel useless
in the blank face of it all.

And yet, my daughter still makes me smile
  and my son makes me laugh.

Yet the girl who was raped, she would not stop tickling her
brother,
    both of them lost in joy.

Yet the girl with the HIV scabs all over her body on the dirty
streets of Kampala,
    she could not stop her giggling and pulling faces at me,
    her revelry a refusal in the face of the disease
    that burned through her body.

Yet the boy from Burma who had just seen his family shot,
he still loved
    to play paper, rock and scissors; he would beat me every time.

Yet the children still chase each other daily
    through the bombed-out buildings of a broken city.
They do not realise, so they do not let the delight die.

Yet they fly kites.
Yet they dance.
Yet they dream.
Yet the mothers still sing
    and I have heard their song
    and it sounds like hope
    and it sounds like revelry.

I do not understand it.

But joy still resides here, somewhere,
    between the spaces of suffering
    and amidst the affliction,
    and beneath the hurting
    and within the wretched.

Where joy should not be,
there she thrives
more vibrant than anything.

So if they, those pressed-down friends,
  if they may smile in the grim face of it all,
then I too must find a place of gladness, even as I stand beside
  them,
lest I deny them the delight they have to feel.

To honour who they are,
  I too must appreciate the way the sun rises always with colour.
  I too must find the flowers growing like hope in the gardens.
  I too must savour the taste of these words on my tongue.
  I too must hold hands with delight and kiss the extravagant,
revel in the beauty of this existence. To not despair, to see that
  beauty,
she is everywhere, folded deep into every dark thing.

  I too must believe that the God who created this world
        did not make it bland nor tasteless,
        but full. So full. So very full.

Friends, do not despair, for life and beauty and joy and truth,
        they are everywhere,
        folded deep into every dark thing.

~

... let us throw off everything that hinders and the sin that so easily entangles. And let us run with perseverance the race marked out for us, fixing our eyes on Jesus, the pioneer and perfecter of faith. For the joy set before him he endured the cross, scorning its shame, and sat down at the right hand of the throne of God. Consider him who endured such opposition from sinners, so that you will not grow weary and lose heart.

(Hebrews 12:1–4)

~

Epilogue

> I am called here to grow. 'Death' is a critical point of growth, a transition to a new mode of being, to a maturity and fruitfulness that I do not know (they are in Christ and His kingdom). The child in the womb does not know what will come after birth. He must be born in order to live. I am here to learn to face death as my birth ...
>
> **Thomas Merton**[98]

Giving birth is never an easy task. Never a walk in the park, nor hands held in soft moonlight. It is, rather, a backbreaking task, a sweat-in-the-eye task. Actually, I am not even sure it should be called a 'task'. That word is too easy, too everyday. It should be called a toil. A grindstone. A splinter. A sorrow. It should be called a confrontation. A deliberation. A disturbance. It should be called a cocoon – the moment where nothing can ever remain the same.

In April 2014 my wife gave birth to our son. The day before she went into labour, the Saturday, was the day I finished writing the first draft of the first version of this manuscript. Two pregnancies found birth in one weekend. I am sure one was substantially more painful than the other. In the same few days, they made their way out into the world. I had held these words and she had held him.

Two years later, on 28 March 2016, came our daughter. I got to see her first breath. Her literal first breath – life filling her lungs for the very first time. I have never seen anything so sacred before.

Breath brings life,
    like pulse brings life,
    like words bring life,
    like life grows whether we choose for it to do so or not.

Both of my children were born on Easter weekend. Appropriate. The way of descent before new life comes.

Indeed, there seems always some form of death before a
   resurrection,
     the labour before the birth,
     the blood before the being,
     the agony before the joy.

The ragged breath of pushing a baby.
The first breath of screaming child.
There is always a suffering path.
Always a tearing.

The Easter story upholds the weaving together of what most see
   as polar opposites.
     Death and Life.
     Sorrow and Joy.
     Fear and Love.
Two powers that play out over and over.

The days of my children's births were accompanied by Easter death. Easter death accompanied by resurrection life. Red flows in the beginning and in the end. Pain is the constant, but so is beauty. So is love. So is hope.

Pain that leads to death and pain that leads to life: I have seen both. New life will always outweigh the pain of our suffering.

This book began with death. A mother losing her baby and the digging of a small grave in the jungle of Thailand. It ends with the birth of my own children. We have come full circle.

The digging of a grave as a child left the world somehow mirrored what it was to stand helpless beside my wife in the agony of bringing our son into the world. I stood beside the grieving Burmese mother – a sorrow. I stood beside my wife – an opening to newness. I stood beside the tomb of death; I stood beside the womb of life. The grave of sorrow and the womb of new birth are never as separate as we would desire. Both are a beginning and an ending, a sealing and a tearing. They are woven.

I laid the boy's body into the grave with tears of grief falling to the rich earth.

I picked up the body of my baby with tears of joy falling to the sterile hospital floor.

And in the between-time, between the womb and the tomb, there is the stuff of life. Mirroring both its origin and its final destination. The earth opens up a space for our lives where we may touch the beauty and the pain of all that makes us human. It is all here between the first breath and the last. Nothing does not belong.

We are made of 'aching-pain'; we are made of 'delicious-hope'.[99]

The day after digging the grave in Thailand, we were taken to a nearby set of waterfalls. The water was crystal clear and cascading down nature-sculpted stone. We dived down into the depths of the dark water and swam underneath the falls to come up behind them. A cave was nestled in behind the curtain. I screamed. The sight was so overwhelming that I had no other way to express the emotion I was feeling. The exuberance of beauty. The cave was full of crystallised rock, and the sun was just at the right place in the sky to shine through the falling water and strike the formations in the cave. The whole place shone, dazzled, a cave of wonders. The water roared and the light bounced and scattered and glittered. It was the most beautiful explosion of magic I have ever seen.

The day before had been death and sorrow and the digging of a grave; the very next was sheer beauty and delight.

This is life. This is reality. Death and birth held together. Faith and doubt. Sorrow and joy. Hope and despair. Love and fear. Shadow and light. The womb and the tomb. Side-by-side, all the way through. I think back through the moments, the ones that really matter, and there they are again, pressing against each other: burying a child; fleeing in a car with a weeping addict; buying a man a bed; reading John O'Donohue for the first time; placing myself under the ashen waters of the Murrindindi River; walking the Pilgrims' Way out to the Holy Island; listening to the lament of the poet; sitting at the McKerrow family table; seeing a woman struck across the face in Papua New Guinea; weeping for a sex slave I had to leave behind; washing dishes with a street worker; spending a weekend with Merton.

The church that sculpted my Faith; the reality that unravelled it; the slow reweaving.

My life will always be a great intermingling of that which is still sculpted within me, that which has unravelled and that which has found a new weave. These three realities will always remain. From one fishbowl into another. From rebellion, to stumble, to fall, to getting back up again. Over and over. Even as I am filled with doubt, I am also filled with hope at who we are and who we can become. I will not let go of either.

These are the stories of my life. And you too hold both these realities inside your own bones. Death and life. Aching pain and delicious hope. The stories of your life are filled with the same juxtaposition. Your faith is filled with the same juxtaposition.

The Sculpted, the Unravelled, the Woven – all that is in you knows these two edges.

They are there in the way we are *sculpted* by family and fishbowls and kitchen tables. The pressure of friends and parents and churches to be who they want us to be and the all-consuming force of the media machine. The labels we place on ourselves and the names that hold us captive. The places we call home. The roles we live out and the traditions we have escaped from. And the traditions we have escaped *to* – the things we now believe as Truth. The incongruency of our rhetoric and our reality. The push from our nests of safety.

They are there in the *unravelling* of our story. The wild and the critical. The pointing fingers and the walking out the front door. The tearing of the new from the old. The dissatisfaction. The rebellion. The demanding of answers. The pain of falling hard. The pull of the cynical. The love of a nurturing community and the fear of turning from it. The fear of moving forward. The death of what has been. The life that comes in the discoveries. The love that walks alongside. The mystery of God.

They are there in the *woven*, in the finding of a new weave. The surrender. The open arms. The letting go. The letting others in. The sitting in paradox. The connection with all things. The remembering. The reframing where faith finds its footing. The land that calls you friend. The rivers that speak. The slowing down to find presence and truth and life and God. The imagination to hope for an alternative vision. The wandering through the inner landscapes. The messy spirituality. And grace. Always the grace.

214

It all fits here. None of your life is not worthy. It all comes together. We are woven and this world is woven and the people are woven and God is woven, and this all comes together. This is our hope and our trajectory.

So may you sit in the tension of all that life throws at you and intentionally find a weave within and a weave without. May every fibre of your existence be woven in with the other. In the mundane realities, may you find the wonder. In the pain, may you find the beauty. There is a way forward regardless of the season. Your faith may not look like it once did, but it is yours. So you do not need to throw the baby of faith out with the bathwater of the old. Your faith is a new wellspring, and it holds the joy and the doubt and the grief and the hope. Arms stretched out, it holds them: cruciform. The womb and the tomb. Death before resurrection.

The world spins and the seasons come and go, and age grows, and choices are made, and suffering and beauty come amid spit and laughter and deep lungfuls of life – and I wonder what you will do with it all. The honour and glory and pain of being human: what will you do with it?

You are alive for a time and given the freedom to become. Who will you become? Who will you be in this world of ours?

And who will *we* become? This world. This social existence. Who will we be in this reality of ours? The honour and glory and pain of being human: what will *we all* do with it?

The world is crumpled and fractured and bruised and broken. We all know this. We can see the destruction and oppression and greed all around us. But I must believe that this will change, and that this *is* changing. That a world so twisted can one day be untwisted. While everything in existence now seems to move towards death, my hope is that it will one day move towards life. That light will break into this darkness and bring a glorious sunrise.

The Christian faith calls this New Creation: when the dream that God has for this world comes to total fruition. It is when the old order of patriarchy and domination and oppression and greed is wrung out of this place and, as the old African American spiritual says, we will 'study war no more.' This is when beauty and justice and equality and fairness and goodness will be seen in all things.

This is the future, the tomorrow we are hoping for. But it is also the tomorrow we must join with God to bring about. Through the way we plough the field and plant the seeds. Through the way we eat the toast and drink the wine. Through the way we build our houses and shelter the lonely and stand with those whose voices need to be heard. Through design and media and technology and business and government. Through what we do with our rubbish and the way we talk to our neighbours and our children and our bosses and the guy on the street. Through making art and writing books and performing poetry. Through family and relationships and social media. Through shopping and caring and listening and hoping.

We are a people called from ahead. The long arms of this glorious vision reach out to pull us up into something much larger than ourselves. Something to hang our lives on. This beautiful vision.

This is the grand cathedral we are called to lay the bricks for.

This is the grand tapestry our lives may be woven into, all things knitted back together where they have been so torn apart.

Woven in one beautiful, glorious work of art.

How do we live a life in which our world may be woven back together?

~

Weaving is all about time. Weaving is time made visible. Whenever I sit down at the loom (even after 47 years), I say to myself, 'This is going to take the rest of my life!' I am almost overwhelmed by the enormity of the task, but I keep repeating it like a mantra, over and over. Finally, there comes a moment when I know it is absolutely OK for this particular weaving to take the rest of my life (a moment of total surrender). It is at that moment that I notice I have finished the weaving. It happens every time! It's one of my favourite things about weaving – the ability to make time malleable.

A weaver[100]

~

A Boat Story (continued)

The girl was given a boat. A wooden boat. A small boat for a small girl.

She cast it off from the sandy shore. Her dad was standing right beside her, cheering her on. He had built her the boat and taught her everything he knew about the ocean.

Now it was her turn. The day had come. After years of practice it was time for her to set sail from the home she had always known.

The night before, her father had sat her down and told her a story. It was about a harbour and chasing a dolphin and a storm and getting lost and a broken boat that had almost sunk, and it was about how he had rebuilt the boat out there in the waters from the flotsam and jetsam.

He told her that it was 10 years of sailing before he had found that harbour again. And that when he did, his own father had dropped everything and run out into the water to greet him with wide open arms. He had stayed for a short time before setting sail once more. But he made sure he still went back to visit.

He told her that should she find herself in a similar place, lost and alone and far from home in a storm and an ocean she did not recognise, he knew she would be OK if she remembered what he had taught her. He told her that he would be waiting for her, always. If she came back in a week or a month or in 10 years or never, he would always be there for her.

The girl's hands were shaking, but she was determined. She pushed the boat out into the water, jumped inside, turned the bow towards the horizon and waved to her father. Then she hoisted the sail and was off to wherever and whatever lay ahead.

Acknowledgments

I began writing this book on the Holy Island of Lindisfarne in 2012, but it brings together learnings and experiences from the last 18 years of my life. There is no way I can name everyone who has inputted into the content and stories found in these pages. So this is a huge thanks to all who were there at the beginning during my sculpting years; to my mum and dad for the table you made for us McKerrow kids – you have always loved us well, and I am so thankful; to the many friends and influences and role models during my teenage and emerging adult years; to all who journeyed with me through the unravelling and all who since have helped me find a reweaving; to those who listened and wrestled and discussed with me the concepts and how to best bring them to the world; to all my students who have put their trust in the thoughts and ideas and heart of this fellow pilgrim. Thank you all for your input into my life.

There are, however, a few people whom I cannot go without naming. Rowan Lewis and Mia Kiaferis: you have been as iron to sharpen iron over the many, many years of journeying alongside young people. This would not be a book without you both. Your fingerprints are on every page. Luke and Sarah Hawkins: you have been there from the beginning, and it is an absolute joy to still have you in my life and see who you two have become. Thank you, too, to my fellow creative conspirators and dear friends Anna Weir, Joy Prouty and Richelle Bourne: you have all been such a huge support for me these past years and I am so thankful for you.

It is seven years since Lindisfarne, and over that time so many different people have helped bring this book together. Vickie Reddy: thank you for connecting me with the wonderful Lisa and all your other fantastic friends throughout the world. Lisa Jackson from Alive Literary Agency: a huge thank you for your incredible efforts in working with this manuscript all the way from the USA and being so supportive of its potential to change people's lives. Belinda Rule: thank you for the very first edit through the first version of this manuscript. A huge thanks also to Kristin Argall, Susannah McFarlane, John Sandeman and the team at Acorn Press and Bible Society Australia for being willing to take this book on board and birth it into the world. To my editor Owen Salter and the design team and everybody else who had a part in the production, thank you!

Lastly, to my wife and children – those closest to me who know my intricacies and my foibles. I will never be able to express what it means to have you by my side. Thank you for being there through it all. For teaching me to be a better human. For loving me when I do not do this life well. For holding me when I stumble. For making me laugh. I love you.

Notes

1   J. O'Donohue, *Eternal Echoes: Celtic Reflections on Our Yearning to Belong*, HarperCollins, New York NY, 1999, pp. 13, 15.

2   Quoted in J. Lederach, *The Moral Imagination: The Art and Soul of Building Peace*, Oxford University Press, New York, NY 2005, p. 114.

3   Cited on website *Today in Science History®*, viewed 8 April 2019, as follows: In 'Gravity quantized?', *Scientific American*, vol. 267, no. 3, 1992, pp. 18–19. As quoted in Clifford A. Pickover, *Wonders of Numbers*, OUP, 2003, p. 195. https://todayinsci.com/W/Wheeler_John/WheelerJohn-Quotations.htm.

4   Quoted in J. Hand, *Women, Power and the Biology of Peace*, Questpath Publishing, San Diego, 2003, p. 130.

5   N. Marlens & C. Black (writers), *The Wonder Years*, Pilot Episode 1x01, Original airdate 31 January 1988, New World Television, 1988.

6   T. Campolo & B. McClaren, *Adventures in Missing the Point*, Zondervan, Grand Rapids MI, 2003, p. 61.

7   Trefis Team, 'Trends in Global Advertising Industry: Winners and Losers – Part 1', *Forbes*, 28 September 2015, viewed 8 April 2019, https://www.forbes.com/sites/greatspeculations/2015/09/28/trends-in-global-advertising-industry-winners-and-losers-part-1/#19470a7350ac.

8   J. Koblin, 'How Much Do We Love TV? Let Us Count the Ways', *New York Times*, 30 June 2016, viewed 8 April 2019, https://www.nytimes.com/2016/07/01/business/media/nielsen-survey-media-viewing.html.

9   J. Simpson, 'Finding Brand Success in the Digital World', *Forbes*, 25 August 2017, viewed 8 April 2019, https://www.forbes.com/sites/forbesagencycouncil/2017/08/25/finding-brand-success-in-the-digital-world/#22f249be626e.

10   Quoted in R. Timkin, 'Brands are the new religion, says ad agency', *Financial Times*, March 2004.

11   A. Storkey, 'Postmodernism Is Consumption', in C. Bartholomew & T. Moritz (eds), *Christ and Consumerism*, Paternoster Press, Cumbria UK, 2000, p. 100.

12   E.O. De Bary, *Theological Reflection: The Creation of Spiritual Power in the Information Age*, Liturgical Press, Collegeville MN, 2003, p. 25.

13   J. Wallis, *God's Politics*, Harper, San Francisco, 2005, p. 36.

14   J. Kavanaugh, *Following Christ in Consumer Society* (25th Anniversary Edn), Orbis, New York NY, 2006, p. 10.

15   W. Mueller, *Engaging the Soul of Youth Culture*, Intervarsity Press, Downers Grove IL, 2006, p. 219.

16 R. Gibson, *How Shall We Live as Lambs Among Wolves? Reason – Passion – Power – Organization*. Keynote lecture delivered at Rouge Forum Conference, Louisville, KY, 2008, www.richgibson.com/rouge_forum/2008/lambsamongwolves.htm (viewed 12 April 2019).

17 J. Moltmann, *Religion, Revolution and the Future*, Scribner's, New York NY, 1969, p. 142.

18 Aboriginal Activists Group, Queensland, 1970s. See http://unnecessaryevils. blogspot.com/2008/11/attributing-words.html.

19 A. Zierman, *When We Were on Fire*, Convergent Books, New York NY, 2013, p. 42.

20 Quoted in R. Webber, *The Younger Evangelicals*, Baker Bookhouse, Grand Rapids MI, 2002, p. 135.

21 Like the passage that speaks of the 'most outstanding of the apostles [the church leaders]' being a woman named Junia (Romans 16:7).

22 L. Harper, keynote talk at The Justice Conference, Melbourne, November 2018.

23 M. Frost & A. Hirsch, *The Shaping of Things to Come*, Hendrickson Publishers, MA/ Strand Publishing, Erina, NSW, 2003, p. 50.

24 K. Dean, C. Clark & D. Rahn, *Starting Right: Thinking Theologically about Youth Ministry*, Zondervan, Grand Rapids MI, 2001, p. 28.

25 Attributed to Kierkegaard in *Journal of Marriage and Family Therapy*, vol. 2, 1976, American Association for Marriage and Family Therapy, p. 33 (no earlier incidents have been located).

26 S. Bessey, *Out of Sorts: Making Peace with an Evolving Faith*, Darton, Longmann and Todd, London UK. 2015, p. 1.

27 Dory is the forgetful Blue Tang fish from the movie *Finding Nemo*..

28 K. Gibran, *The Prophet*, Penguin First Vintage Books edn, Penguin, London UK, 2015, p. 4.

29 Z. Braff (dir.), *Garden State*, Camelot Pictures, Jersey Films, Double Feature Films, 2004.

30 M. Newell (dir.), Mona Lisa Smile, Revolution Studios/Columbia Pictures, 2003.

31 V. van Gogh, from his 'Letters to Theo', 29 December 1881, viewed 8 April 2019, http://vangoghletters.org/vg/letters/let194/translation.html.

32 R. McKee, *Story*, Methuen Publishing, London UK, 1998, p. 181.

33 R. Rohr, *Adam's Return: The Five Promises of Male Initiation*, The Crossroad Publishing Company, New York NY, 2004, p. 136.

34 Quoted in R. Ferguson, *A Real-Life Christian Spiritual Journey*, AuthorHouse, Bloomington IN, 2011, p. 125.

35 Found in B. Kolodiejchuk, 'Aspects Revealed by Mother Teresa's Process of

Beatification and Canonization', viewed 30 April 2019, http://www.corpuschristi movement.com/english/meditations/Fr.%20Brian%20on%20Mother.pdf.

36   R.M. Rilke, *Letters to a Young Poet*, Penguin Books, London, 2012 (Kindle edn).

37   D. Fincher (dir.), *Fight Club*, Twentieth Century Fox, 1999.

38   J. Drane, *The McDonaldization of the Church*, Darton, Longman & Todd, London, 2000, p. 5.

39   For a revealing look at this, see http://storyofstuff.org.

40   Kavanaugh, *Following Christ in Consumer Society*, p. 60.

41   L. Tolstoy, *What Then Must We Do?* Element Books, n.p., 1991, p. 73.

42   N.T. Wright, *How God Became King: The Forgotten Story of the Gospels*, Harper Collins, New York NY, 2012, pp. 44–45.

43   NITV, 'Indigenous life expectancy 'worst in the world'', 15 January 2010, updated 1 February 2017, viewed 8 April 2019, http://www.sbs.com.au/nitv/article/2010/01/15/indigenous-life-expectancy-worst-world.

44   B. Fryer, 'Indigenous youth suicide at crisis point', NITV News, 15 January 2019, viewed 8 April 2019, https://www.sbs.com.au/nitv/article/2019/01/15/indigenous-youth-suicide-crisis-point?cx_navSource=related-side-cx#cxrecs_s.

45   Ibid.

46   Australian Institute of Health and Welfare, *Australia's Welfare 2017: In Brief*, 19 October 2017, viewed 8 April 2019, https://www.aihw.gov.au/reports/australias-welfare/australias-welfare-2017-in-brief/contents/indigenous-australians.

47   Ibid.

48   Quoted in J. Dear, *Peace Behind Bars: A Peacemaking Priest's Journal from Jail*, Sheed & Ward, Kansas City MO, 1995, p. 65.

49   A. Zierman, *When We Were on Fire*, p. 147.

50   L.F. Winner, *Still: Notes on a Mid-Faith Crisis*, HarperCollins, New York NY, 2013, pp. xv, 8, 15.

51   Ibid., p. xvii.

52   R.A. Wilson, *The Illuminatus Trilogy*, Constable & Robinson, London, 1998, p. 462.

53   J. McKerrow, *These Wandering Feet: Reflections from a Travelling Pilgrim*, Poatina Tree Publications, Melbourne, p. 35.

54   P. Reps (comp.), *Zen Flesh, Zen Bones*, viewed 7 May 2019, https://terebess.hu/zen/101ZenStones.pdf.

55   Rumi, *The Essential Rumi*, C. Barks (trans.), Harper Collins, New York NY, 2004, p. 152.

56   D. Miller, *A Million Miles in a Thousand Years*, Thomas Nelson, Nashville TN, 2011, p. 68.

57 E. Fromm, *Man for Himself: An Inquiry into the Psychology of Ethics*, Henry Holt & Company, New York NY, 1947, p. 46.

58 D. Kinnamen, *You Lost Me: Why Young Christians Are Leaving the Church ... and Rethinking Faith*, Baker Publishing Group, Grand Rapids MI, 2011, p. 23.

59 Steve Martino (dir.), *Dr Seuss' Horton Hears a Who!* (film), Blue Sky Studios/ Twentieth Century Fox, 2008.

60 Winner, *Still: Notes on a Mid-faith Crisis*, p. xiv.

61 V. van Gogh, 'Letters to Theo', c. 23 December 1881, 23 November 1881, viewed 9 April 2019, http://www.vangoghletters.org/vg/letters/let189/letter.html, http://vangoghletters.org/vg/letters/let193/letter.html.

62 J. O'Donohue, *Eternal Echoes: Celtic Reflections on Our Yearning to Belong*, HarperCollins, New York NY, 1999.

63 W. Brueggemann, *The Land: Place as Gift, Promise and Challenge in Biblical Faith*, Fortress Press, Philadelphia PA, 1977, p. xii.

64 M.L. King, *A Gift of Love*, Beacon Press, Boston MA, 2012, p. 18.

65 A. Solzhenitsyn, *The Gulag Archipelago*, Collins, London, 1974, p. 168.

66 A. Nowlan, *Between Tears and Laughter*, Clarke Irwin, Toronto, 1971, p. 102.

67 See the videos of these poems, 'Confession Series', at www.joelmckerrow.com.

68 S. Kumar, 'From Ownership to Relationship', *Resurgence*, Issue 235, March/April 2006, viewed 8 April 2019, https://www.resurgence.org/magazine/article440-from-ownership-to-relationship.html.

69 Quoted in N. Beirma, *Bringing Heaven Down to Earth*, P&R Publishing, Phillipsburg NJ, 2005, p. 157.

70 Quoted in J. Wallis, *Faith Works: Lessons from the Life of an Activist Preacher*, Random House, New York NY, 2000, p. xvii.

71 A. Hutchinson, *In Memory of Reverend Father Damien, J. De Veuster and Other Priests Who Have Laboured in the Leper Settlement of Kalawao*, Sacred Hearts Archives, Leuven, Belgium, 1931, pp. 3–4.

72 Quoted in B. Vogt, 'A Leper for Christ: St Damien of Molokai and Solidarity', *Word on Fire Blog*, 10 May 2016, viewed 8 April 2019, https://www.wordonfire.org/resources/blog/a-leper-for-christ-st-damien-of-molokai-and-solidarity/2274.

73 M. Quinlan & R.L. Stevenson, *Damien of Molokai*, McDonald & Evans, London, 1909, p. 136.

74 Quoted in H. Thompson, '#InContext: Dietrich Bonhoeffer', The Human Trafficking Institute, 1 November 2017, viewed 8 April 2019, https://www.traffickinginstitute.org/incontext-dietrich-bonhoeffer.

75 H. Thielicke, *I Believe – The Christian's Creed*, Fortress Press, Philadelphia PA, 1968, p. 35.

76 Zierman, *When We Were on Fire*, p. 220.

77 Quoted in R. Rohr, *Falling Upward: A Spirituality for the Two Halves of Life*, Jossey Bass, San Francisco, 2011, p. 112.

78 Frost & Hirsch, *The Shaping of Things to Come*, pp. 132, 147.

79 Quoted in Frost & Hirsch, *The Shaping of Things to Come*, p. 130.

80 M. Yaconelli, *Messy Spirituality*, Zondervan, Grand Rapids MI, 2007, p. 13.

81 Taken from *The Message: The Bible in Contemporary Language*, a paraphrase of the Bible by Eugene H. Peterson, NavPress, 2002.

82 J. Keats, 'Letter to George and Georgiana Keats', 14 February to 3 May 1819, viewed 8 April 2019, http://www.john-keats.com/briefe/140219.htm.

83 T. Merton, *New Seeds of Contemplation*, New Directions, New York NY, 2007, p. 3.

84 T. Merton, *The Intimate Merton: His Life from His Journals*, HarperOne, New York NY, 2001, p. 265.

85 Ibid., p. 364.

86 Ibid., p. 313.

87 E. Underhill, *Practical Mysticism for Normal People*, Dent, London, 1914, p. 23.

88 F. MacEowen, *The Mist-Filled Path*, New World Library, Novato CA, 2010, p. 8.

89 Brother Lawrence, *The Practice of the Presence of God*, Baker Book House, Grand Rapids MI, 1958, p. 30.

90 J. Vanier, *Community and Growth*, Griffin House, Toronto, 1979, p. 102.

91 Quoted in A. Voskamp, *One Thousand Gifts*, Zondervan, Grand Rapids MI, 2010, p. 131.

92 T. Moore, *The Re-Enchantment of Everyday Life*, Harper Perennial, New York NY, 1997.

93 P.G. Blanton, 'Adding Silence to Stories: Narrative Therapy and Contemplation', *Contemporary Family Therapy*, 29(4):211–221, December 2007.

94 M. Eckhart, *Meister Eckhart Selected Writings*, Sermon 16, Penguin Books, London, 1994, p. 179.

95 P. Rollins, *How (Not) to Speak of God*, SPCK Publishing, London, 2006, p. 148.

96 M. Laird, *Into the Silent Land*, Oxford University Press, New York NY, 2006, p. 9.

97 Ibid., p. xxxv.

98 Merton, *The Intimate Merton*, p. 317.

99 R. Rolheiser, *The Holy Longing*, Crown Publishing, New York NY, 2014, p. 5.

100 Bonnie, 'Time to Weave', *Weaving Spirit*, 15 February 2007, viewed 8 April 2019, https://weavingspirit.blogspot.com.au/2007/02/time-to-weave.html?m=0, 2007.

About the Author

Joel McKerrow is an award-winning writer, speaker, educator and community arts worker. He is one of Australia's most successful internationally touring performance poets, having performed for hundreds of thousands of people around the world since 2010. Based in Melbourne, Australia, he is the artist ambassador for the aid and development organisation TEAR Australia and the co-founder and co-host of the podcast *The Deep Place: On Creativity and Spirituality.*

Joel was also the co-founder of community arts organisation *The Centre for Poetics and Justice* (2010–2013), was the third-ever Australian representative at the Individual World Poetry Slam Championships in the USA (2012) and has previously released three music/spoken word albums as well as three published books of poetry.

Alongside his writing and poetry, Joel is a highly sought-after speaker at conferences, schools, colleges, churches and gatherings all over the world. His speaking focuses on the intersection of spiritual formation, social justice, creativity and identity. This comes after walking alongside young people for the last 18 years in schools, churches, youth work organisations and theological institutions, through which he has become known worldwide as an experienced practitioner and thinker in these areas of personal formation. He is currently a lecturer at Whitley Theological College where he helps run a program of spiritual formation for 17–25-year-olds, and he also spends much of his time performing/speaking/teaching in schools throughout Australia.

Joel loves to wood carve in the little spare time he has and, with his wife and two children, is a member of Eastern Hills Community Church in Melbourne, Australia.

www.joelmckerrow.com